AF675778

PLYMOUTH COLONY PROBATE GUIDE

Where to find Wills and Related Data

For 800 People of Plymouth Colony

1620 -- 1691

Compiled by

Ruth Wilder Sherman, FASG

Robert S. Wakefield, FASG

PLYMOUTH COLONY RESEARCH GROUP

Publication Number Two

1983

Withdrawn from the Collections
of the
Montgomery County Historical Society

The Montgomery County Historical Society
103 West Montgomery Avenue
Rockville, Maryland 20850

929.3
MA
She

copyright 1983

PLYMOUTH COLONY RESEARCH GROUP

128 Massasoit Drive, Warwick RI 02888

Ruth Wilder Sherman, Production Editor

First Printing, August 1983

Library of Congress Cataloging in Publication Data

Sherman, Ruth Ann Wilder 1929-
Plymouth Colony probate guide.

(Publication / Plymouth Colony Research Group ; no. 2)
Bibliography: p.
Includes index.
1. Pilgrims (New Plymouth colony)--Genealogy.
2. Massachusetts--Genealogy. 3. Probate records--
Massachusetts. 4. Rhode Island--Genealogy. 5. Probate
records--Rhode Island. I. Wakefield, Robert S.,
1925- . II. Title. III. Series: Publication
(Plymouth Colony Research Group) ; no. 2.
F63.S53 1983 929'.1'072074 83-2362
ISBN 0-910233-01-2

Printed in the United States of America

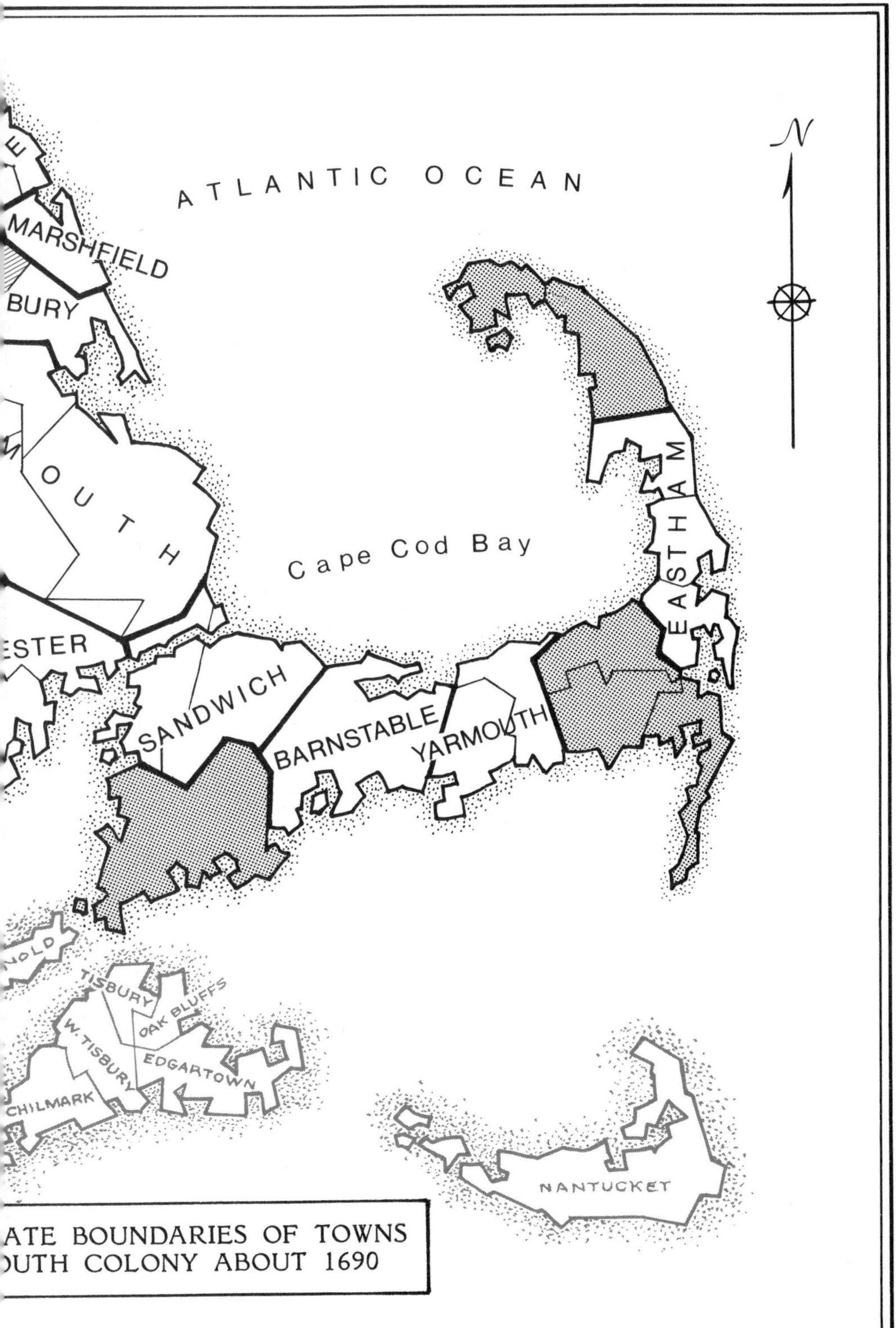

ATE BOUNDARIES OF TOWNS
UTH COLONY ABOUT 1690

in memory of

CLAUDE WILLIS BARLOW, FASG

1907-1976

A valued genealogical friend

3170

TABLE OF CONTENTS

Introduction vii

Plymouth Colony Probate Sources ix

What This Guide Contains xiii

Probate Act Under Andros xv

Acknowledgements xvii

Plymouth Colony Research Group xix

About The Authors xxi

PLYMOUTH COLONY PROBATE GUIDE 1

Index to Other Names in the Guide 123

Other Published Probate Records 133

Key to Abbreviated Titles 155

Where to Obtain Books and Journals 165

INTRODUCTION

PLYMOUTH COLONY, long known simply as the Old Colony, came into being in 1620 with the arrival of the Pilgrims from England, and lasted until absorbed by Massachusetts Bay Colony in October 1691. During those seven decades the Colony encompassed most of the area now lying within three southeastern counties of Massachusetts -- Barnstable, Bristol, and Plymouth -- and also portions of two adjacent counties of Rhode Island -- Bristol and Newport.

Of those adult Plymouth Colony residents who died before 1692, less than one-fifth left any sort of probate record. The bulk of this material is found in Colony records. A significant additional portion is found in records of the counties of Barnstable, Bristol, and Plymouth, all of which were incorporated in 1685. Furthermore, because the law stipulated that all Colony estates of more than £50 value probated during the term of Sir Edmund Andros as Royal Governor of the Dominion of New England (1686-1689), and also during the final years of the Colony (1689-1691) were to be handled at Boston, these are found in the records of Suffolk County.

The largest single published source of Colony records is _Records of the Colony of New Plymouth_, by Nathaniel B. Shurtleff and David Pulsifer, published in the middle of the last century. Their work has since been supplemented, and at times corrected or duplicated, by George Ernest Bowman in _The Mayflower Descendant_ and _Pilgrim Notes and Queries_, and by Lucy Hall Greenlaw in _The Genealogical Advertiser_.

From the above, one may better understand why it is no simple matter for genealogists, historians, and others involved in Plymouth Colony research to locate the probate documents which interest them. The situation will, in time, be alleviated by publication of the records mentioned above through the efforts of three non-profit corporations. In the 1960s the Research Department of Plimoth Plantation began transcribing all wills and related records. About the time of our country's Bicentennial, Dr. Anne E. Yentsch joined the Plantation's research staff, and directed the continued gathering, transcribing and editing of documents for publication. The work has been financed from several sources: the revolving publication fund of the Massachusetts Society of Mayflower Descendants, grants to Brown University from the National Endowment for the Humanities, and continued support from the Plantation. Although the monumental work is nearing completion, and microfiche of the work may become available in a year or so, publication in book form is still several years away. Until that time, researchers must still consult the scattered published materials, and the microfilmed originals.

This Guide is, indirectly, a by-product of the above project which, at one time, was to include a brief biographical note with each set of probate documents. To assure that the notes were prepared from suitable published sources, Robert Wakefield and I volunteered to provide a list of such sources. As our work progressed, the idea occurred to publish an enhanced list in a separate volume, to make available more quickly this information about the 800 Plymouth Colony men and women who left probate records.

To all of the published and unpublished materials mentioned above, this slim volume is a particular guide.

Warwick, June 1983 Ruth Wilder Sherman, FASG

PLYMOUTH COLONY PROBATE SOURCES

NOTE: All sources listed below have been microfilmed by the Genealogical Society of Utah, genealogical arm of the Church of Jesus Christ of Latter Day Saints (the Mormons), and are available through its branch libraries around the world.

Records of Plymouth Colony

The following volumes are in the custody of the Plymouth County Register of Deeds, but at this time are held in the county vault, in the office of the County Commissioners, in the annex to the Plymouth County Court House.

4 volumes labelled "Wills." Contemporary official record books containing copies of original wills and many other probate matters.

> PUBLISHED: All of volumes 1 and 2, and part 1 of volume 3 through page 153, sometimes in abstract, in *Mayflower Descendant* (MD) volumes 1-34; most probate items from MD pertaining to Mayflower passengers have been reprinted in *Mayflower Reader* (MAY RDR), and some of these appear in *Mayflower Quarterly* (MQ).

1 volume labelled "Scrapbook." A bound collection of those few original Colony wills and related materials still owned by Plymouth County, which survive today. Some of these, particularly the bonds of administrators, were not copied into the record books, and are occasionally our only sources for residences or names of wives of men listed in this Guide. (There are also some original documents owned by the Pilgrim Society of

Plymouth MA, and by the Massachusetts Society of Mayflower Descendants, which are transcribed in MD and their ownership therein identified. Not all of these were copied into the Colony record books.)

PUBLISHED: In its entirety, as The Plymouth Scrapbook (PLYM SCRAP).

12 volumes: six labelled "Court Orders"; one "Indian Deeds, Accounts and Freemen"; three "Acts of the Commissioners of United Colonies of New England"; one "Laws"; and one "Marriages, Births and Deaths." These are contemporary official record books containing copies of original records, including scattered probate matters and copies of a few wills, reports of inquests, etc.

PUBLISHED: In their entirety, as volumes 1-11 of Records of the Colony of New Plymouth (PLYM COL RECS).

11 volumes labelled "Deeds." Contemporary official record books containing copies of deeds, and a smattering of probates (mostly in volume five) including several wills.

PUBLISHED: Volume 1 of these deeds was published as volume 12 of PLYM COL RECS; all of volume 2, and part of volume 3, through page 27, are abstracted in MD volumes 1-34, and include those recorded as late as 1655.

*

Some probate records of the colony period are found in the following counties which were formed in 1685.

Probate Records of Barnstable County

The following records are located on the second floor of the Barnstable County Court House, Barnstable, Mass.

Original papers burned; most probate record books were saved and have been Xeroxed for use. Index gives name of decedent, town of residence, type of document, year action was taken, and volume and page.

PUBLISHED: Abstracts of all of volume 1, and volume 2 through page 119, in MD volumes 2-34.

Probate Records of Bristol County

The following records are located on the second floor of the Bristol County Registry of Deeds, Taunton, Mass.

Many original papers, filed alphabetically by name of decedent; earliest cases not numbered. Record books in good condition. Index, which covers record books only, gives name of decedent, type of document, and volume and page.

PUBLISHED: Volume 1 through page 49 in _Genealogical Advertiser_ (GEN ADV) 3-4; some in _New England Historical and Genealogical Register_ (NEHGR) volumes 62-64.

Probate Records of Plymouth County

The following records are located on the second floor of the Plymouth County Registry of Deeds, Plymouth, Mass.

Many original papers, filed by case number. Record books in good condition. Alphabetical dockets provide index to books and original papers, and give name of decedent, town of residence, type of document, date of action taken, file number, and volume and page number.

PUBLISHED: Volume 1 through page 69, and some original papers, in PN&Q volumes 4-5; volume 1, to page 237, abstracted in GEN ADV volumes 1-4; some abstracted in NEHGR volumes 4-7.

*

Probate Records of Suffolk County

The following records are located in the Probate Office on the first floor of the old Suffolk County Court House, opposite Government Center, Boston, Mass.

From 1686 to 1691, Plymouth Colony probate records for estates valued at more than £50 appear in this county (see page xv). There are many original papers, case numbered. Old series record books in worn condition. Published indexes give name, type of document, year, and probate file number; dockets give name of decedent, year estate was probated, type of document, volume and page in record book, and note if original documents are missing. Often the town of residence is stated.

> PUBLISHED: Some early records abstracted in NEHGR volumes 2-48. A list of estates probated during the Andros administration appears in TAG volumes 12-14.

There are also some probate matters in the original court records and record books on the 14th floor of the new Suffolk County Court House, opposite Government Center, Boston, Mass.

> PUBLISHED: Suffolk County Court Records from 1671-1680 in volumes 29-30 of _Publications of the Colonial Society of Massachusetts_.

WHAT THIS GUIDE CONTAINS

IN THIS GUIDE we have gathered information concerning more than 725 men and 75 women -- everyone for whom we found probate material in the Plymouth Colony records, and also every Colony resident for whom we could find probate records elsewhere. The earliest probate records in Colony books is dated 1633. This Guide encompasses all probates, known to the authors, for Colony residents who died from the time of the landing of the Pilgrims in 1620 through 31 December 1691, although Plymouth Colony actually went out of existence in October 1691. For definitions of legal terminology, see _The Researcher's Guide to American Genealogy_, Val D. Greenwood (1973). Square brackets in the text enclose editorial comments by the authors, which do not appear in the original records.

For each individual we list the following, when available, and if known to the authors:

1. Town of residence, if given in the probate record, otherwise from one of the other cited references. A few individuals left so little evidence that it is impossible to determine their residences.

2. The relationship of the person or his spouse to a _Mayflower_ passenger.

3. Name of ship on which the person arrived, if immigration occurred during the busy 1620-1624 period.

4. The relationship of the person to some other person in this Guide, in many cases.

5. The year the will was signed, if there was a will; in all cases, the year of the earliest action on the estate.

6. Name of spouse, if in the probate record, otherwise that of closest relative named in probate record; if no relative named, then the name of a person or persons involved with the estate.

7. Settlement of the estate on an heir, or division of real or personal property among the heirs.

8. Every reference found by the authors for each person, when he or she is the subject of probate, in published and unpublished sources which are described in the previous pages. However, where estates contain several documents, only the most genealogically significant are named in the Guide. The published sources, almost without exception, cite the original documents from which they were taken.

9. Sources of all information, in brief form. See Key to Titles for full bibliographical citations.

10. A biographical citation, the last reference in each entry (after the phrase "for further information see also") lists further selected references, of which many are still in print and most are available in genealogical collections and libraries. Family genealogies are not included, since they are usually the first place researchers will look. Sources are primarily those which are less obvious and more difficult to search, such as periodical literature and town histories. Most of the people appear in SAVAGE, but his work is generally cited only when the authors found no other references.

NOTE: This Guide was not planned to be a complete listing of all references about each person mentioned. One important source which may have further references on families is New England Marriages Prior to 1700 by Clarence A. Torrey. This multi-volume manuscript, at New England Historic Genealogical Society, has been microfilmed, and is available in this form at some libraries, such as the New York Genealogical and Biographical Society. Readers should also consult the genealogical periodical indexes, beginning with the three volumes by Jacobus, and the more recent volumes of Genealogical Periodical Annual Index.

PROBATE ACT UNDER ANDROS

THE ACT signed by Edmund Andros which caused certain Plymouth estates to be probated at Boston is pertinent to this volume, but not readily found in print. For this reason we print the act below, exactly as it appears in Laws of New Hampshire, Albert S. Batchellor, editor, 1904, 1:206.

[Chapter 11]

An Act for probate of Wills & Granting Letters of Administration.

[This act is printed from the original in the Massachusetts files. Passed June 1, 1687, 3 James II. Colonial Records of Connecticut, vol. 3, p. 423.]

BEE ITT ENACTED by the Governor and Councill And Itt is Enacted and ordained by the Authority of the same That the probate of all wills and l'res of Adminstrac'on shall be from Hencefforth granted by the Governor or such person as he shall Commissionate under the seale of the office for that purpose Appointed And that All wills Relateing to any Estate within the severall Countyes of Suffolk and Midds' shall be proved at Boston before the Governor or such p'son a shall be Commisc'onated as aforesaid But in Regard of the Remotenesse of other Countyes from the said place And to prevent the Charge of Bringing Witnesses soe farr each Inferiour Court of Com'on Pleas shall and are hereby Impowred to take the Examinac'on of witnesses to any will within their Respective Countys upon oath and the same with the will to Certifye to the secreataryes office at Boston with all Convenient Speed under the Hand of the Judge and Clarke of the said Court That the probat thereof may be granted Accordingly And on Extraordinary occac'ons or Necessity the Judges of the Inferriour Courts Assisted with two Justices of the peace within the said Remote Countyes may and Are hereby Impowred at any tyme out of Court to take the Examinac'on of Wittnesses to any will to be produced before them upon Oath and to Certifye the same as aforesaid And in case any Debate or Controvercy Shall Arise About sweareing and Examn'ng such Wittnesses or allowing the will The said Court or Judge and Justices may heare and Determine the same And if any be unsatisfied with their proceedings therein they may Appeale to the Governor or such other person Comissionated as aforesaid before the probate of Such will be granted.

AND ITT IS FURTHER ENACTED and Ordained that the severall Judges of the Inferriour Courts within the said Remote Countyes in Open Court or on Extraordinary occac'on or Necessity out of Court assisted with two Justicies of the peace Aforesaid may and Are hereby Authorized and Impowred to grant probates of any will or Letters of Administracc'on to any person or [per]sons where the Estate of the person Makeing such will or of the Intestate on which letters of Administrac'on is Desired Doeth not Exceed the vallue of ffifty pounds Anything herein before Contained to the Contrary hereof in any wise not withstanding.

PROVIDED always that any person or p'sons Concerned in the Probate of such will or letters of Administrac'on to be Granted by the Judg of the Inferriour Courts As aforesaid may within three mon[t]h After the Granting thereof bring his or their Appeale or Appeales therein before the Governor or such other [per]son Commissionated As Aforesaid

Councill Chamber in Boston the ffirst day of June in the third yeare of his Ma'ties Reigne Annoq'e D'ni 1687.

E Andros.

By Ord'r of the Governor
and Councill
John West, D. Sec'ry.

ACKNOWLEDGEMENTS

THE AUTHORS acknowledge a debt to the following:

George Ernest Bowman, that indefatigable genealogist of the Pilgrim period who transcribed, or wrote, or edited much of the published material to which we make reference herein. Also the Massachusetts Society of Mayflower Descendants for their George Ernest Bowman Collection which provided a number of clues for research.

Jane Fletcher Fiske, Robert S. Trim and Alicia Crane Williams, all of whom we consulted about various aspects of this volume, and who gave generously of their comments.

Our colleagues, Robert C. Anderson, Roger D. Joslyn and Robert M. Sherman, who examined the text closely; their suggestions were most valuable to us.

William White Sherman, without whose computer expertise we could not have put together this, our first totally computer-produced hard-cover volume.

Cynthia Hagar Krusell of Marshfield, Louise H. Kelley of Harwich, Walter Babbitt of Brewster, and Russell Lovell Jr. of Sandwich, who were consulted about the 1690 end-paper map.

Charles F. Mathewson of Noonan-Leyden Press, for artwork.

PLYMOUTH COLONY RESEARCH GROUP

We are an informal group of genealogical researchers with strong interests in Old Plymouth Colony from its origin in 1620 to its incorporation in Massachusetts Bay Colony in 1691 (although our research will occasionally stray beyond these boundaries of time and place). We plan to put forth, from time to time, publications which we hope will be of value to others with similar interests; these publications will include indexes, research aids, source material and compiled genealogies.

Robert Charles Anderson FASG
Roger D. Joslyn FASG
Robert M. Sherman FASG
Ruth Wilder Sherman FASG
Robert S. Wakefield FASG

ABOUT THE AUTHORS

RUTH WILDER SHERMAN is author or editor, with her husband Robert Moody Sherman, of _Marshfield_ and _Yarmouth Mass. Vital Records_ (1969 & 1975), co-author of "The William White Family" in volume one of _Mayflower Families Through Five Generations_ (1975), and editor of several other volumes, including _Peleg Burroughs's Journal 1778-1798: the Tiverton R.I. Years of the Humbly Bold Baptist Minister_ (1981). She is known for her articles on Plymouth Colony and Colonial Rhode Island families, appearing principally in _The American Genealogist_, of which she is a Contributing Editor. She is a Certified Genealogist and a Fellow of the American Society of Genealogists.

ROBERT SIDNEY WAKEFIELD is author of _Plymouth Colony Marriages to 1650_ (1978) and co-author of "The Richard More Family" in volume two of _Mayflower Families Through Five Generations_ (1978), and is researching another Mayflower Family -- Peter Brown. He is known for his articles on Colonial Rhode Island and Massachusetts families, appearing principally in _The American Genealogist_, of which he is a Contributing Editor. He is a Fellow of the American Society of Genealogists. He has just retired as supervisor of a large staff of computer programmers in Northern California for the Southern Pacific Transportation Co.

PLYMOUTH COLONY PROBATE GUIDE

1620-1691

ABELL

ROBERT of Rehoboth; 1663 inventory (MD 15:239); 1663/4 administration granted to widow Joanna (PLYM COL RECS 4:46, 54); for further information see also MA PIONEERS p. 9, WEYMOUTH BY CHAMBERLAIN 3:5

ADAMS

JAMES, residence unknown; 1652 inventory exhibited by Kenelm Winslow of Marshfield (MD 11:10); for further information see also TAG 55:212

JOHN of Plymouth; came on the ship Fortune; 1633 inventory (MD 1:157); 1633 division names his widow Ellen Adams (PLYM COL RECS 1:19); for further information see also TAG 24:71-73, 55:212

ALCOCK

JOHN of Roxbury; son of George; 1666 will mentions deceased unnamed wife and his mother[-in-law] Palsgrave (PLYM COL PR 3:2:64); for further information see also SAVAGE 1:21

ALDEN

JOHN Sr. of Duxbury; came on the ship Mayflower; 1687 inventory, sworn by son Jonathan, and receipts of heirs (MD 3:10, MAY RDR p. 151, GEN ADV 1:18-19); for further information see also FAMS OF PILGRIMS, MD 3:120, BRIDGEWATER BY MITCHELL p. 83, DUXBURY BY WINSOR p. 213, TAG 53:235

ALLEN/ALLYN

GEORGE the elder of Sandwich; undated will proved 1649 names wife Catherine (MD 9:224); for further information see also MA PIONEERS pp. 13-14, TAG 36:64, WEYMOUTH BY CHAMBERLAIN 3:11, CAPE COD HIST 2:46

ALLEN/ALLYN con't

JOHN of Scituate; nuncupative will, 1662 inventory sworn by widow Ann Allen (MD 17:218); estate settled (PLYM COL RECS 4:28, 35, 39, 81, 89); for further information see also MA PIONEERS p. 14, SCITUATE BY DEANE p. 212, BARNSTABLE FAMS 1:12

JOHN of Swansea; 1689/90 Bristol Co. will names wife Christian (GEN ADV 3:121); for further information see also SWANSEA TR A:147

ROBERT; brother of John of Rehoboth; 1661 report of his death (PLYM COL RECS 3:221); 1661/2 inquest (PLYM COL RECS 4:9, 13)

THOMAS of Barnstable; 1675 will names son Samuel, 1680 inventory (PLYM COL PR 4:1:49); for further information see also MA PIONEERS p. 15, CAPE COD HIST 2:274, LECHFORD'S NOTEBOOK p. 421 [original p. 229], BARNSTABLE FAMS 1:5

WILLIAM of Prudence Island [now in Portsmouth RI]; 1685 will names wife Elizabeth (Portsmouth RI PR 1:241); for further information see also SWANSEA HIST p. 140, RI GEN DICT p. 2, TAG 48:224

ALMY

JOHN of [the Island of] Rhode Island; 1676 dower set off to widow Mary (PLYM COL RECS 5:212-3); 1679 letter re estate (PLYM SCRAP pp. 10-11); for further information see also RI GEN DICT p. 238, RI FAMS 1:312

AMMIDOWN see ANNADOWN

ANDREWS

HENRY of Taunton; 1652/3 will names wife Mary (MD 11:152); 1664 payment to his daughter (PLYM COL RECS 4:70); for further information see also MA PIONEERS p. 18

HENRY of Taunton; son of Henry; 1676 inventory; undated settlement mentions unnamed widow (PLYM COL PR 3:2:28, 66-67); 1678/9 division of his estate (PLYM COL RECS 6:5); for further information see also MA PIONEERS p. 18

ANDREWS con't

MARY of Taunton; 1653 will mentions deceased husband Henry (MD 12:246); for further information see also MA PIONEERS p. 18

ANNABLE

ANTHONY of Barnstable; came on the ship Anne; 1672 will names wife Ann, 1674 codicil (MD 25:90); 1674 oath to inventory (PLYM COL RECS 5:146); for further information see also MA PIONEERS p. 19, CAPE COD HIST 2:272, BARNSTABLE FAMS 1:13, SCITUATE BY DEANE p. 213

SAMUEL of Barnstable; son of Anthony; 1678 inventory sworn by widow Mehitable Annable (PLYM COL PR 3:2:129); settlement (PLYM COL RECS 5:272); for further information see also MA PIONEERS p. 18, BARNSTABLE FAMS 1:18

ANNADOWN/AMMIDOWN

ROGER of Rehoboth; 1673 inventory (MD 25:122); 1673/4 inquest (PLYM COL RECS 5:141); 1673 bond of widow Joanna Ammadown as administratrix (PLYM SCRAP p. 115); 1673/4 settlement (PLYM COL RECS 5:138-139); for further information see also MA PIONEERS p. 17 (under Ammidown), WEYMOUTH BY CHAMBERLAIN 3:13

ATWOOD see also WOOD

ANN; 1650 will drawn at New Plymouth, proved 1654, names deceased husband John (MD 11:200); for further information see also MA PIONEERS p. 23

JOHN of Plymouth; 1643 will, exhibited 1644, names wife Ann (MD 5:153); for further information see also MA PIONEERS p. 23

AUDEY

WEBB of Plymouth; 1651/2 will bequeaths to the church, and the town poor (MD 11:8); for further information see also MA PIONEERS p. 24, PLYM COL RECS 12:35

AUSTIN

JONAS Jr. of Taunton; 1676 inventory sworn by widow Esther Austin (PLYM COL PR 3:2:26, 57); for further information see also MA PIONEERS p. 24

BABBITT see BOBBETT

BACON

ELIZABETH, probably of Barnstable; daughter of Nathaniel; undated will exhibited 1676/7 (PLYM COL PR 3:2:59); for further information see also MA PIONEERS p. 26

NATHANIEL Sr. of Barnstable; 1673 inventory (MD 24:134); 1673 administration granted to Mistress Hannah Bacon (PLYM COL RECS 5:134); 1673 bond of administrators (PLYM SCRAP pp. 115-116); 1673 settlement (PLYM COL RECS 5:137); settlement (PLYM COL LR 3:128, 324); for further information see also MA PIONEERS p. 26, TAG 57:103-108, BARNSTABLE FAMS 1:21

NATHANIEL of Barnstable; 1691 Barnstable Co. will, probated 1692 names wife Hannah (MD 2:215); for further information see also MD 2:215, TAG 45:60

BAILEY see BAYLEY

BAKER

NICHOLAS of Scituate; son of Nicholas; 1678 will names wife Grace (PLYM COL PR 3:2:133); for further information see also MA PIONEERS p. 28, SCITUATE BY DEANE pp. 181-2, TAG 27:95, BARNSTABLE FAMS 1:60

BANGS

EDWARD Sr. of Eastham; came on the ship Anne; agreement and 1677 will which names son Jonathan Bangs executor (PLYM COL PR 3:2:105-106); for further information see also MA PIONEERS p. 31

BARKER

ISAAC of Duxbury; 1688/9 Suffolk Co. inventory says he died 14 Feb. 1689, administration granted to widow Judith Barker (SUFFOLK CO. PROBATE OLD SERIES 10:562, 13:3, NEW SERIES 1:222); 1693 Plymouth Co. settlement (GEN ADV 3:93); for further information see also SAVAGE 1:115

BARKER con't

JOHN of Marshfield; 1652 inventory (MD 11:156, PLYM SCRAP p. 11); 1653 inquest (PLYM COL RECS 3:28); 1653 administration granted to his widow Anna Barker (PLYM COL RECS 3:37); 1660-1668 receipts of heirs (MD 17:111); for further information see also MA PIONEERS p. 32, BARNSTABLE FAMS 1:64, SCITUATE BY DEANE p. 216

JONATHAN of Middleboro; 1690 Plymouth Co. inventory sworn by widow Jane Barker (MD 31:18, GEN ADV 2:89)

BARLOW

GEORGE of Sandwich; 1684 will mentions unnamed wife (PLYM COL PR 4:2:82); inventory sworn by sons John and Nathan (PLYM SCRAP p. 51); for further information see also MA PIONEERS pp. 32-3, CAPE COD HIST 2:63

BARNABEY

JAMES of Plymouth; married Lydia Bartlett, granddaughter of Pilgrim Richard Warren; 1677 settlement names widow Lydia, who is about to marry John Nelson (PLYM COL RECS 5:247); 1677 inventory (PLYM COL PR 3:2:98); son choses guardians (PLYM CO CT RECS 1:199); for further information see also FAMS OF PILGRIMS (Warren family), TAG 56:34

BARNES

JOHN of Plymouth; 1667/8 will names wife Joan (MD 4:98, PLYM SCRAP p. 56); 1671 administration (PLYM COL RECS 5:81); inventory (PLYM SCRAP pp. 102-108); 1671/2 inquest (PLYM COL RECS 5:88); for further information see also MA PIONEERS p. 33, EARLY REHOBOTH 1:80

BARRELL/BARRILL

WILLIAM of Scituate; 1688/9 Plymouth Co. inventory sworn by widow Lydia Barrill (MD 19:145 or GEN ADV 1:75 or PN&Q 5:90); for further information see also SCITUATE BY DEANE p. 217, BRIDGEWATER BY MITCHELL p. 108, NEHGR 87:200

BARSTOW/BERSTOW

JEREMIAH of Scituate; 1679 administration granted to his brother John Barstow (PLYM COL RECS 6:23); in 1677 and 1679 the widow, Lydia, wife of Richard Stanlake, was appointed guardian of her sons by Barstow (PLYM COL RECS 5:235, 6:23); for further information see also SCITUATE BY DEANE p. 218, MA PIONEERS p. 35 errs in calling Lydia the widow of John Barstow

WILLIAM of Scituate; 1668/9 administration granted to Anna Barstow (PLYM COL RECS 5:13); inventory (MD 17:116); for further information see also MA PIONEERS p. 36, SCITUATE BY DEANE p. 218, SCITUATE BY PRATT p. 342

BARTLETT

BENJAMIN of Duxbury; grandson of Pilgrim Richard Warren; his first wife was probably Sarah Brewster, granddaughter of Pilgrim William Brewster; 1691 Plymouth Co. will names wife Sissilla [or Cecily] (MD 6:44, GEN ADV 2:91-92, 3:26); son choses guardian (PLYM CO CT RECS 1:210); for further information see also FAMS OF PILGRIMS (Brewster and Warren families), DUXBURY BY WINSOR p. 225, BRIDGEWATER BY MITCHELL p. 376

JOHN of Rehoboth; 1684 inventory (PLYM COL PR 4:2:149); 1684/5 administration granted to widow Sarah Bartlett, who died before she could administer (PLYM COL RECS 6:153); for further information see also NARRA HIST REG 6:30 or RI FAMS 1:123

MOSES late of Boston; died Mannamoy; master of a boat owned by Joseph Peirse of Boston (PLYM COL RECS 6:4) 1678 inventory (PLYM COL PR 4:1:7)

ROBERT of Plymouth; came on the ship Anne; married Mary daughter of Pilgrim Richard Warren; 1676 will mentions unnamed "wife" (MD 3:114); 1676/7 administration granted to Mary Bartlett and Joseph Bartlett (PLYM COL RECS 5:220); for further information see also FAMS OF PILGRIMS (Warren family), TAG 35:214, 55:164, MD 3:105, BRIDGEWATER BY MITCHELL p. 376; MA PIONEERS p. 36

BARTRUM
WILLIAM of Swansey; 1688 Bristol Co. will names wife Sarah (GEN ADV 4:58); for further information see also SAVAGE 1:134

BASSETT
WILLIAM Sr. of Bridgewater; came on the ship Fortune; 1667 will, with wife Mary swearing to inventory (MD 16:162, PLYM SCRAP pp. 57-59); for further information see also MARTHA'S VINEYARD BY BANKS 3:30, MA PIONEERS p. 37 (which may be confusing two men), BARNSTABLE FAMS 1:45, BRIDGEWATER BY MITCHELL p. 111, DUXBURY BY WINSOR p. 226, TG 3:165

WILLIAM of Sandwich; 1670 inventory (MD 18:253, PLYM SCRAP p. 57); will proved (PLYM COL RECS 5:43); 1670 administration granted to Mistress Mary Bassett (PLYM COL RECS 5:47); 1670/1 guardianships for children (PLYM COL RECS 5:52); for further information see also MARTHA'S VINEYARD BY BANKS 3:31, MA PIONEERS p. 37 (which may be confusing two men), BARNSTABLE FAMS 1:47

BATSON
Child; 1678 inquest on unnamed child of Anne (Winter) Batson, probably of Marshfield (PLYM COL RECS 5:260-2); for further information see also MARSHFIELD VR p. 8

BAYLEY
GUIDO Jr. of Bridgewater; son of Guido; 1690 Plymouth Co. inventory sworn by administrator Ebenezer Hill (GEN ADV 1:114 or PN&Q 5:115); for further information see also TAG 33:138

BEADLE see BIDDLE

BEARE see also BEERE
RICHARD of Marshfield; 1673 will names Richard French executor (MD 25:90); for further information see also MA PIONEERS p. 42, DUXBURY BY WINSOR p. 227

BEARSE see BEERE

BEERE

ROBERT of Rehoboth; married Elizabeth (Billington) Bullock, granddaughter of Pilgrim John Billington; 1677 inventory (PLYM COL PR 4:2:46); for further information see also TAG 39:65, TG 3:228ff, FAMS OF PILGRIMS (Billington family),

BELL

JAMES of Taunton; 1676/7 inventory (PLYM COL PR 3:2:90, PLYM SCRAP p. 124); 1677 settlement to Esther Marshall (PLYM COL RECS 5:235); for further information see also SAVAGE 1:159

BENT

JOSIAH of Marshfield; 1686 guardianship for his son Joseph (GEN ADV 1:17); for further information see also MARSHFIELD VR p. 5, SAVAGE 1:169

BERRY

RICHARD of Yarmouth; 1681 will (PLYM COL PR 4:1:101); inventory names widow Alice Berry (PLYM COL RECS 6:101); for further information see also MA PIONEERS p. 47, YARMOUTH BY SWIFT p. 72, BARNSTABLE FAMS 1:136

BERSTOW see BARSTOW

BERTRAM see BARTRUM

BESBEY

ELISHA Sr. of Marshfield; 1688 will names son Hopestill Besbey executor, 1690 Plymouth Co. inventory (GEN ADV 1:114 or PN&Q 5:116); for further information see also MA PIONEERS p. 47, HINGHAM BY LINCOLN 2:82 (Bisbee family), DUXBURY BY WINSOR p. 227 (Bisbee family)

BESSEY

ANTHONY of Sandwich; 1656 will, proved 1658, names wife Jane (MD 14:152); for further information see also MA PIONEERS p. 47, TAG 26:193, CAPE COD HIST 2:74, BARNSTABLE FAMS 1:69 (footnote)

BEWITT

GEORGE of Sandwich; 1675 will names minister John Smith executor (MD 34:114); for further information see also MA PIONEERS p. 77 (Buitt family)

BIDDLE
JOSEPH of Marshfield; 1671 will, exhibited 1672, names wife Rachel (MD 19:163); for further information see also PLYM COL MARR p. 4, SAVAGE 1:175

BILLINGTON
THOMAS of Taunton; not of the Mayflower Billington family; 1662 testimony re his will (MD 17:216); 1662 administration granted to James Leonard of Taunton (PLYM COL RECS 4:16); for further information see also NEHGR 6:243, TG 3:243

BIRAM see BYRAM

BIRD
THOMAS of Scituate; 1663/4 will names wife Ann (MD 16:123); 1681 claim on estate by Peter Worthylake (PLYM COL RECS 6:66); for further information see also MA PIONEERS pp. 50-51, SCITUATE BY DEANE p. 221

BISBEE see BESBEY

Blacks see TOOTO

BLACKLEICH
SOLOMON, commander of the frigate James; 1678 will mentions but does not name his wife in "Catalina," possibly the port of that name in Newfoundland (PLYM COL RECS 5:267-270)

BLACKMORE
WILLIAM of Scituate; 1676 administration granted to widow Elizabeth Blackmore, with settlement (PLYM COL RECS 5:211); inventory (PLYM COL PR 3:2:13); for further information see also SCITUATE BY DEANE p. 221

BLACKSTONE
WILLIAM of Study Hill [now Cumberland RI]; 1675 inventory (PLYM COL PR 3:1:173); settlement to stepson John Stevenson (PLYM COL RECS 5:172); guardians for son John Blackstone named (PLYM COL RECS 5:181); for further information see also MA PIONEERS p. 53, NEHGR 15:315, EARLY REHOBOTH 3:69, RI GEN DICT p. 21, RI ROOTS 8:51, WEYMOUTH BY CHAMBERLAIN 3:96

BLACKWELL

JOHN of Sandwich; married Sarah Warren, granddaughter of Pilgrim Richard Warren; 1688 Barnstable Co. settlement to widow Sarah Blackwell (MD 10:7); for further information see also NEHGR 117:184, FAMS OF PILGRIMS (Warren family)

BLISH see BLUSH

BLISS

JONATHAN Jr. of Rehoboth; 1687 Suffolk Co. bond by son Jonathan (SUFFOLK CO. MA PR #1629); 1688 quitclaim by eldest son Samuel (BRISTOL CO LR 1:104); for further information see also SAVAGE 1:200

THOMAS of Rehoboth; 1647 will names son Jonathan and son-in-law Thomas Willmore [or Willmarth] executors (MD 8:85); 1648 petition for portion of the estate (PLYM COL RECS 2:126); for further information see also MA PIONEERS p. 55

BLOSSOM

THOMAS of Barnstable; 1650 inventory (MD 10:21); 1650 administration granted to his widow Sarah (PLYM COL RECS 2:156); for further information see also MA PIONEERS p. 56, BARNSTABLE FAMS 1:75

BLUSH/BLISH

ABRAHAM of Barnstable; 1682 will names wife Alice (PLYM COL PR 4:2:126); will sworn 1683/4 (PLYM COL RECS 6:123); for further information see also MA PIONEERS p. 368, PLYM COL PR 4:2:32, BARNSTABLE FAMS 1:89

BOARDMAN see BORDMAN

BOBBETT

EDWARD Sr. of Taunton; 1676/7 inventory (PLYM COL PR 3:2:56); 1676/7 administration granted to widow Sarah Bobbett with settlement (PLYM COL RECS 5:217-8); 1684 administration granted to Edward Bobbett (PLYM COL RECS 6:132-3); for further information see also MA PIONEERS p. 57

BOND

JOHN of Plymouth; servant to George Watson; 1661 inquest (PLYM COL RECS 3:223)

BORDMAN

THOMAS of Yarmouth; 1689 Barnstable Co. will names wife Elizabeth (MD 10:101-2); for further information see also YARMOUTH BY SWIFT p. 75

BOREMAN see BURMAN

BOSWORTH

NATHANIEL of Bristol (now RI); 1689/90 Bristol Co. will, 1690 administration granted to widow Bridget Bosworth (GEN ADV 3:122)

BOURMAN see BURMAN

BOURNE

ALICE; wife of John of Marshfield; 1686 administration (PLYM COL RECS 6:184); for further information see also John of Marshfield below

JOB of Sandwich; 1676/7 settlement to widow Ruhamah (PLYM COL RECS 5:218, PLYM COL LR 4:74); inventory (PLYM COL PR 3:2:48); for further information see also NEHGR 118:197, BARNSTABLE FAMS 1:111

JOHN of Suffolk Co.; 1674 bond of John Cann as administrator (PLYM SCRAP p. 121); for further information see also SUFFOLK CO. PROBATE #725

JOHN of Marshfield; 1684 will (PLYM COL PR 4:2:89); 1686 administration on estates of John and wife Alice granted to son Thomas Bourne (PLYM COL RECS 6:184); Plymouth Co. division of estate (GEN ADV 1:17 or PN&Q 4:2); for further information see also MA PIONEERS p. 59, PN&Q 4:3

RICHARD of Sandwich; 1682 settlement names widow Ruth Bourne, 1682 administration (PLYM COL RECS 6:97); settlement (PLYM COL PR 4:2:1); for further information see also NEHGR 118:83, SAVAGE 1:218, BARNSTABLE FAMS 1:104

BOURNE con't

SARAH; widow of Henry of Barnstable; incomplete and undated will recorded in the same hand as the will following it, which was recorded after 1684/5 [not in Plymouth Co. or Barnstable Co. PR] (PLYM COL PR 4:2:84); for further information see also MA PIONEERS p. 59

THOMAS of Marshfield; 1664 will names son John Bourne executor (MD 16:24); for further information see also MA PIONEERS p. 60, MARSHFIELD BY RICHARDS 2:177

BOWEN

RICHARD Sr. of Rehoboth; undated will, exhibited 1675, names wife Elizabeth (MD 17:247); 1674 bond of administrator (PLYM SCRAP p. 117); for further information see also MA PIONEERS p. 60

THOMAS, late of New London, Connecticut, "sojourning in Rehoboth"; 1663 will names wife Elizabeth (MD 16:128); for further information see also SAVAGE 1:223, RI FAMS 1:139

WILLIAM of Rehoboth; 1687 Bristol Co. administration granted to Richard Bowen (GEN ADV 3:119); agreement between his brothers Richard and Obadiah (BRISTOL CO LR 1:66-67)

BOWMAN see BURMAN

BRADFORD

ALICE Sr. of Plymouth; widow of Gov. William Bradford; came on the ship <u>Anne</u>; 1669 will (MD 3:144 or MAY RDR p. 194); for further information see also FAMS OF PILGRIMS

WILLIAM Sr. of Plymouth; came on the ship <u>Mayflower</u>; Governor of Plymouth Colony; 1657 will names wife Alice (MD 2:228 or MAY RDR p. 139); for further information see also FAMS OF PILGRIMS, MQ 27:4:6-7, 35:10, MD 7:65, DUXBURY BY WINSOR p. 230, BRIDGEWATER BY MITCHELL p. 377, TAG 46:117, 47:87, NEHGR 83:439-464, 84:5-17

BRADFORD con't

WILLIAM of Plymouth; grandson of Pilgrim William; 1687 inquest (PLYM CO CT RECS 1:190); Plymouth Co. administration granted to John Bradford (GEN ADV 1:18 or PN&Q 4:4); in 1700 his children chose guardians (MD 16:115); for further information see also FAMS OF PILGRIMS, MD 9:115, BRIDGEWATER BY MITCHELL p. 378

BRADLEY

THOMAS, singleman of Portsmouth RI; 1653 inquest (PLYM COL RECS 3:39)

BRENTON

WILLIAM of Newport RI; 1673 will names son Jahleel executor (MD 34:75); for further information see also MA PIONEERS p. 19, RI GEN DICT p. 252

BRETT/BRITT

WILLIAM Sr. of Bridgewater; 1681 will names wife Margaret (PLYM COL PR 4:1:106); 1681/2 inventory sworn (PLYM COL RECS 6:81); for further information see also MA PIONEERS p. 67, BRIDGEWATER BY MITCHELL p. 120, DUXBURY BY WINSOR p. 234

BREWSTER

LOVE of Duxbury; son of Pilgrim William Brewster; Love also came on the ship Mayflower; 1650 will names wife Sarah (MD 2:203 or MAY RDR p. 135 or MQ 28:4:10); for further information see also FAMS OF PILGRIMS, BRIDGEWATER BY MITCHELL p. 381, DUXBURY BY WINSOR p. 235

NATHANIEL of Duxbury; son of Love; 1676 testimony of his brother Wrestling re will (PLYM COL PR 3:2:40); 1676 administration granted to Robert Vixon of Eastham (PLYM COL RECS 5:212); for further information see also FAMS OF PILGRIMS

WILLIAM of Plymouth; came on the ship Mayflower; 1644 inventory (MD 3:15 or MAY RDR p. 153); settlement (PLYM COL RECS 12:115); administration granted to Jonathan and Love Brewster (PLYM COL RECS 2:73); for further information see also FAMS OF PILGRIMS, NEHGR 124:250, TAG 41:1, 63, BRIDGEWATER BY MITCHELL p. 381, DUXBURY BY WINSOR p. 234, NEHGR 113:235, 128:288, MQ 36:55

BRIANT see BRYANT

BRIGGS

FRANCES of Scituate; wife of Walter; 1687 Plymouth Co. administration granted to her sons John Rogers and Joseph Rogers (GEN ADV 1:19 or PN&Q 4:107, PLYM COL RECS 6:134); for further information see also SCITUATE BY DEANE p. 225

JOHN of Sandwich; 1641 settlement (MD 3:224); administration granted to his widow Katherine Briggs (MD 3:224, PLYM COL RECS 2:18); for further information see also MA PIONEERS p. 69

JOHN of Scituate; 1687 Suffolk Co. bond of widow Deborah Briggs as administratrix (SUFFOLK CO. PROBATE #1603, OLD SERIES 10:402); for further information see also SCITUATE BY DEANE p. 225

JONATHAN of Taunton; son of Clement; 1688/9 Bristol Co. administration granted to son Jonathan Briggs and widow Experience Briggs, 1690 settlement (GEN ADV 3:118, 121); for further information see also MA PIONEERS p. 68, TAG 33:84

WALTER of Scituate; 1676 will, presented 1684, names wife "Francis" (PLYM COL RECS 6:134-6); for further information see also SCITUATE BY DEANE p. 225, DUXBURY BY WINSOR p. 237

BRITT see BRETT

BROOKES

WILLIAM of Scituate; 1682/3 will names wife Susannah (PLYM COL PR 4:2:21); for further information see also MA PIONEERS p. 71, SCITUATE BY DEANE p. 223

BROWING see BROWNING

BROWN(E)

DOROTHY of Swansea; widow of John Brown Sr. of Rehoboth; 1668 will, exhibited 1673/4, names son John Browne executor (MD 18:94); receipts (GEN ADV 3:120)

JOHN of Duxbury; 1672 will, sworn 1684, names wife Phebe (PLYM COL PR 4:2:128); for further information see also DUXBURY BY WINSOR p. 238

BROWN(E) con't

JOHN Jr. of Wannamoiset [now Swansea]; son of John Sr. below; 1662 will names his father John Browne executor (MD 18:14); receipts (GEN ADV 3:120)

JOHN Sr. of Rehoboth; 1662 will, with inventory sworn by Mistress Dorothy Browne (MD 18:18); receipts of heirs (GEN ADV 3:120); for further information see also MA PIONEERS p. 73, SWANSEA HIST pp. 198-200

PETER of Plymouth; came on the ship Mayflower; 1633 inventory and settlement name his wife Mary (MD 1:79, 5:29 or MAY RDR p. 363); inventory presented (PLYM COL RECS 1:17); provision for his daughters (PLYM COL RECS 1:18-19); for further information see also TAG 42:35, NGSQ 67:253-4

SAMUEL of Eastham; died 1691, 1692 inventory sworn by widow Martha Browne (MD 14:116); for further information see also SAVAGE 1:276

WILLIAM probably of Taunton; 1662 testimony re disposition of his land names cousin Peter Walker (PLYM COL RECS 4:28)

WILLIAM of Bristol (now RI); 1689 Bristol Co. will names John Corps executor (GEN ADV 3:118-9)

BROWNING/BROWING

JOHN of Marshfield; 1653 inquest as Browing (PLYM COL RECS 3:28); division of his estate names Widow Waterman (PLYM COL RECS 3:39)

BRYANT/BRIANT

JOHN the elder of Cohannack (Taunton); 1638 nuncupative will names son John Bryant (MD 2:210); for further information see also MA PIONEERS p. 76

JOHN Sr. of Scituate; 1684 will names wife Mary (PLYM COL PR 4:2:86); for further information see also SCITUATE BY DEANE p. 227

BRYANT/BRIANT con't

SAMUEL of Scituate, Sgt.; son of John Sr.; 1690/1 Plymouth Co. administration granted to his brother John Bryant (GEN ADV 1:116); 1690/1 inventory (MD 30:70); for further information see also SCITUATE BY DEANE p. 228

BUCKE

JOHN of Scituate; 1679/80 administration granted to John Sutton (PLYM COL RECS 6:32); for further information see also SCITUATE BY DEANE p. 229 (article on his father John)

BUCKLAND/BUCKLIN

BENJAMIN, of Rehoboth; son of William; 1676 inventory by Braintree men includes land near Providence RI, 1677 settlement names widow Rachel Buckland (PLYM COL PR 3:2:80); for further information see also MA PIONEERS p. 76

WILLIAM of Rehoboth; 1684 administration granted to Joseph Buckland (PLYM COL RECS 6:146); for further information see also MD 16:82, SAVAGE 1:285, HINGHAM BY LINCOLN 2:96

BULLOKE/BULLOCK

RICHARD of Rehoboth; married (2) Elizabeth Billington, granddaughter of Pilgrim John Billington; 1667 inventory (MD 17:28, PLYM SCRAP pp. 61-62); 1669 petition of widow Elizabeth Bullock and Samuel Bullock (PLYM COL RECS 5:27); 1670 settlements (PLYM COL RECS 5:45, 50); 1677 distribution of estate made with consent of widow Elizabeth, now Widow Bears (PLYM COL RECS 5:233); for further information see also PLYM COL MARR p. 8, TAG 39:65, FAMS OF PILGRIMS (Billington family), TG 3:228ff

BUNDEY

JOHN Sr. of Taunton; married Martha Chandler, granddaughter of Pilgrim James Chilton; 1681 will mentions unnamed wife (PLYM COL PR 4:1:99, Plymouth Co. PR #3310); for further information see also MF 2:12, TAG 37:212

BURG/BURGESS

THOMAS of Sandwich; 1684 will, sworn 1684/5 mentions unnamed "dear wife" and appoints sons Ezra Perry and Jacob Burg executors (PLYM COL PR 4:2:92); for further information see also MA PIONEERS p. 80, LITTLE COMPTON FAMS p. 130, DUXBURY BY WINSOR p. 239, NEHGR 118:323

BURMAN/BOURMAN/BOREMAN

THOMAS of Barnstable; 1663 will, with widow Hannah Burman swearing to inventory (MD 18:63); administration (PLYM COL RECS 4:41); for further information see also PLYM COL MARR p. 6, BARNSTABLE FAMS p. 80; MA PIONEERS p. 57 probably confuses two men

BURROWES

JEREMIAH of Marshfield; 1660 inventory taken by Josias Winslow and William Sherman (MD 17:112); 1660 administration granted to unnamed widow (PLYM COL RECS 3:202); 1660/1 inquest (PLYM COL RECS 3:208); for further information see also MA PIONEERS p. 82, MD 17:186, SCITUATE BY DEANE p. 228, TAG 40:33

JOHN of Marshfield; 1676 inventory and settlement (MD 17:187); 1676 administration granted to Jeremiah Burroughs (PLYM COL RECS 5:201)

BURSELL

JAMES of Yarmouth; 1676 inventory (PLYM COL PR 3:2:61); settlement names widow Emett Bursell (PLYM COL RECS 5:212); for further information see also SAVAGE 1:312

BURSLEY

JOHN of Barnstable; 1660 inventory appraised by John Smith and John Chipman (MD 17:159); for further information see also MA PIONEERS p. 82, PLYM COL MARR p. 8, WEYMOUTH BY CHAMBERLAIN 3:147, BARNSTABLE FAMS 1:127

THOMAS, residence not stated; 1660 division names widow Joanna Bursley (PLYM COL RECS 3:201)

BURT(T)

JAMES Sr. of Taunton; 1677 will, 1680 inventory sworn by James Burt Jr. (PLYM COL PR 4:1:76); for further information see also MA PIONEERS p. 83

BURT(T) con't

RICHARD of Taunton; 1647 guardianship for his son Richard (PLYM COL RECS 2:119); for further information see also MA PIONEERS p. 83

RICHARD of Taunton; 1685 will names wife Charity (PLYM COL LR 5:364-5); for further information see also EARLY REHOBOTH 1:15, 65

BUTTERWORTH

SAMUEL of Rehoboth; 1684 will names cousin John Butterworth executor (PLYM COL PR 4:2:147); for further information see also MA PIONEERS p. 85, WEYMOUTH BY CHAMBERLAIN 3:148

BYRAM

NICHOLAS of Bridgewater; 1687/8 Plymouth Co. will names wife Susanna (GEN ADV 1:20 or PN&Q 4:109); for further information see also MA PIONEERS p. 86, BRIDGEWATER BY MITCHELL p. 127

CALHOUN/CAHOON

WILLIAM of Swansea or Barnstable; in 1681 Joseph Kent and Caleb Lumbart were approved as guardians of Joseph Cahoon, who was probably his son (PLYM COL RECS 6:69); for further information see also MD 21:37, CHARLESTOWN BY WYMAN 1:163

CAREY see CARY

CARPENTER

ABIGAIL; widow of William of Rehoboth; 1686 Bristol Co. inventory and appointment of William Carpenter as administrator (GEN ADV 3:118); for further information see also Rehoboth VR p. 808, MA PIONEERS p. 89

JOSEPH of Swansey; son of William; 1676 [sic] will, with inventory sworn by his widow Margaret Carpenter in 1675 [sic] (PLYM COL PR 3:2:33); 1681 division (PLYM COL RECS 6:66); for further information see also MA PIONEERS p. 89

MARGARET; widow of Joseph; 1676 inventory sworn by William Carpenter, 1677/8 settlement and account (PLYM COL PR 3:2:37, 4:2:121); for further information see also PLYM COL RECS 5:212, 252

SAMUEL Sr. of Rehoboth; son of William; widow Sarah Carpenter swore to 1682/3 inventory (PLYM COL PR 4:2:42); 1682/3 division of the estate (PLYM COL RECS 6:102); 1688 quitclaim of sons (BRISTOL CO LR 1:211-212); for further information see also MA PIONEERS p. 89, EARLY REHOBOTH 1:130, NEHGR 98:170

WILLIAM Sr. of Rehoboth; will dated only "10th month 10th day" makes unnamed wife executrix, 1658 inventory taken by William Carpenter and others (MD 14:231); for further information see also MA PIONEERS p. 89, EARLY REHOBOTH 1:133, WEYMOUTH BY CHAMBERLAIN 3:154

CARVER

JOHN of Marshfield; 1679 inventory sworn by widow Millicent Carver, and undated distribution (PLYM COL PR 4:1:25); for further information see also MARSHFIELD VR p. 5, NEHGR 88:217ff, 119:92

CARY

JOHN Sr. of Bridgewater; 1681 will mentions unnamed wife (PLYM COL PR 4:1:103); 1681/2 administration granted to Sgt. John Carey (PLYM COL RECS 6:81-2); for further information see also MA PIONEERS p. 88, PLYM COL MARR p. 9, BRIDGEWATER BY MITCHELL p. 131, DUXBURY BY WINSOR p. 241

CHACE see CHASE

CHADWELL

RICHARD of Sandwich; 1681 will names son-in-law Lodowick Hawxse executor (PLYM COL PR 4:1:102b); for further information see also MA PIONEERS p. 91

CHAFFEE

THOMAS of Swansea; 1680 will names son Joseph executor, with 1683 inventory (PLYM COL PR 4:2:36, 45); for further information see also MA PIONEERS p. 92

CHAMBERS

RICHARDEN of Scituate, widow; probably married (1) a Curtice; 1672 will proved 1673 names deceased husband Thomas Chambers (MD 24:136); 1673 administration granted to John Curtice (PLYM COL RECS 5:132); for further information see also SCITUATE BY DEANE p. 136

ROBERT of Marshfield "sometimes servant to Mr. Edward Winslow"; 1655 order regarding his estate (PLYM COL RECS 3:88); for further information see also SAVAGE 1:355

CHANDLER

BENJAMIN of Duxborough; son of Edmund; 1691 inventory, settlement, and administration granted to widow Elizabeth Chandler (MD 12:109-110); inventory (GEN ADV 2:106); settlement (PLYM CO CT RECS 1:217); for further information see also DUXBURY BY WINSOR p. 241, SCITUATE BY DEANE p. 231

EDMUND of Duxbury; 1662 will and inventory names son Joseph Chandler executor (MD 14:68); for further information see also MA PIONEERS p. 93, DUXBURY BY WINSOR p. 241

CHANDLER con't

JOHN; 1653 will, "being at sea bound for Barbados," names father Edmund Chandler at New Plimouth (BARBADOS 1:70)

SAMUEL; 1683 Duxbury inventory (MD 14:69, PLYM SCRAP p. 38); 1683/4 settlement, administration granted to "widow" and John Soule (PLYM COL RECS 6:124); inventory (PLYM SCRAP p. 38-39); for further information see also MA PIONEERS p. 93

CHAPELL

ROBERT of Capt. John Allen's company, "put on shore upon Cape Codd"; 1667 inquest (PLYM COL RECS 4:176)

CHAPMAN

RALPH Sr. of Marshfield; unsigned 1671 will names youngest son Ralph Chapman as his heir (MD 19:132); 1673 receipt for legacy (PLYM COL LR 3:306); inventory (PLYM SCRAP p. 110); for further information see also MA PIONEERS p. 94, PLYM COL RECS 5:85, CAPE COD HIST 2:220, RI FAMS 1:193-194

CHASE

MARY of Yarmouth; probably widow of William as their daughter Mary died 1652; 1659 inquest (PLYM COL RECS 3:172); for further information see also MA PIONEERS p. 95, YARMOUTH BY SWIFT p. 59, LITTLE COMPTON FAMS p. 156, NEHGR 87:46

WILLIAM the elder, of Yarmouth; 1659 will, sworn 1659, names wife Mary (MD 17:159); settlement (PLYM COL RECS 3:172); for further information see also MA PIONEERS p. 95, SAVAGE 1:365-6, YARMOUTH BY SWIFT p. 59, LITTLE COMPTON FAMS p. 156, NEHGR 87:46ff, CAPE COD HIST 2:188

WILLIAM of Yarmouth and Dartmouth; 1685 appointment of John Thatcher and Barnabas Lothrop to settle the estate (PLYM COL RECS 6:170); for further information see also SAVAGE 1:365-6, EARLY REHOBOTH 1:46, NEHGR 87:51ff, CAPE COD HIST 2:188

The Montgomery County Historical Society, Inc.
103 West Montgomery Avenue
Rockville, Maryland 20850

3170

CHILD

RICHARD of Marshfield; 1691 administration granted to widow Mary Child, settlement (MD 31:60); administration (GEN ADV 2:90); for further information see also MARSHFIELD VR p. 5, BARNSTABLE FAMS 1:183

CHILLINGSWORTH

THOMAS of Marshfield; 1653 inventory (MD 11:157); 1652/3 administration granted to widow Joan Chillingsworth, 1653/4 settlement (PLYM COL RECS 3:21, 45); for further information see also MA PIONEERS p. 98

CHITTENDEN

ISAAC of Scituate; Martha Chettenden swore to 1676 inventory (PLYM COL PR 3:2:14); administration (PLYM COL RECS 5:211); for further information see also SCITUATE BY DEANE p. 232

THOMAS of Scituate; 1668 will names sons Isaac and Henry executors (MD 17:114); for further information see also MA PIONEERS p. 99

CHURCH

NATHANIEL of Scituate; grandson of Pilgrim Richard Warren; 1689 administration granted to widow Sarah Church (GEN ADV 1:75 or PN&Q 5:91); for further information see also FAMS OF PILGRIMS (Warren family), SCITUATE BY DEANE p. 233, HINGHAM BY LINCOLN 2:126

RICHARD of Hingham; married Elizabeth Warren, daughter of Pilgrim Richard Warren; 1668 will names wife Elizabeth (MD 5:118); for further information see also FAMS OF PILGRIMS (Warren family), HINGHAM BY LINCOLN 2:125, LITTLE COMPTON FAMS p. 166, WEYMOUTH BY CHAMBERLAIN 3:159, BRIDGEWATER BY MITCHELL p. 383, DUXBURY BY WINSOR p. 245

CHURCHILL

JOHN Sr. of Plymouth; 1662 nuncupative will mentions "wife," and names son Joseph Churchill executor (MD 18:40); for further information see also MA PIONEERS p. 79, TAG 36:5, PLYMOUTH TR 1:51, 69, 76

CIVEN

PHILLIP of Scituate; apparently the same as Phillip Phibens; 1685 administration granted to town selectmen (PLYM COL RECS 6:152); for further information see also PHIBENS

CLAGHORN/CLEAGHORN

[ABIGAIL] of Yarmouth; 1677 inquest names husband James (PLYM COL RECS 5:249); for further information see also TAG 52:139

JAMES of Yarmouth; 1683 nuncupative will names eldest son James (PLYM COL PR 4:2:48); for further information see also BARNSTABLE FAMS 1:180, YARMOUTH VR p. 125, MARTHA'S VINEYARD BY BANKS 3:81

CLAPP

ELIEZER of Barnstable; son of Thomas below; 1676 inventory sworn by brother Samuel Clapp, and 1678 settlement (PLYM COL PR 3:1:165, 4:2:119); administration (PLYM COL LR 4:176); receipts (PLYM COL RECS 5:220, 228); for further information see also MA PIONEERS p. 101, BARNSTABLE FAMS 1:249

THOMAS Sr. of Scituate; 1684 will names wife Abigail (PLYM COL PR 4:2:65); for further information see also MA PIONEERS p. 101, SCITUATE BY PRATT p. 306, LITTLE COMPTON FAMS p. 187, WEYMOUTH BY CHAMBERLAIN 3:159

CLARK

FAITH; widow of Thurston; 1663 settlement of estate names her sons Henry and Thurston Clark (PLYM COL RECS 4:39); for further information see also MA PIONEERS p. 103

MARTHA of Plymouth; child of Alice Bishop; 1648 inquest names Alice's husband Richard Bishop (PLYM COL RECS 2:134); for further information see also MA PIONEERS p. 101

THURSTON of Duxbury; 1661 inventory sworn to by widow Faith Clark (MD 17:215); 1661/2 administration, 1662 inquest, estate settlement (PLYM COL RECS 4:8, 12, 39); for further information see also MA PIONEERS p. 103

CLARK con't

WILLIAM of Yarmouth; 1668 nuncupative will leaves estate to Joseph Benjamin (MD 17:109); for further information see also MA PIONEERS p. 104

WILLIAM of Duxbury; 1686/7 Plymouth Co. will names wife Martha (GEN ADV 1:18 or PN&Q 4:4); for further information see also MA PIONEERS p. 104, DUXBURY BY WINSOR p. 247

CLEAGHORN see CLAGHORN

COACHMAN see CUSHMAN

COBB

EDWARD of Taunton; 1675 inventory sworn to by widow Mary Cobb (PLYM COL PR 3:1:172); settlement (PLYM COL RECS 5:179); for further information see also BARNSTABLE FAMS 1:170, SAVAGE 1:413

GERSHOM of Middleboro; son of Henry; 1675 inventory (MD 34:112); settlement names brother John Cobb (PLYM COL RECS 5:180); for further information see also BARNSTABLE FAMS 1:171

HENRY of Barnstable; 1673 will, with 1678 codicil, names wife Sarah, 1679 inventory (PLYM COL PR 4:1:22); for further information see also MA PIONEERS p. 106, SCITUATE BY DEANE p. 238, PLYM COL RECS 8:42, BARNSTABLE FAMS 1:166

JOHN of Taunton; 1690 Bristol Co. will mentions "wife" and names son John executor (GEN ADV 4:60); for further information see also TAG 31:31, 56:106

SARAH of Barnstable; widow of Henry; 1679/80 Thomas Hinckley and Samuel Cobb were granted administration on her estate (PLYM COL RECS 6:32); for further information see also BARNSTABLE FAMS 1:166

COBLEY/COBLEIGH

JOHN of Swansea; 1680/1 administration granted to Jonathan Bosworth Sr. (PLYM COL RECS 6:55); for further information see also PLYM COL RECS 7:214, 8:49, SAVAGE 1:415

COGGEN

HENRY of Barnstable; 1649 inventory sworn by Mrs. Abigail Coggen (MD 9:226, PLYM COL RECS 2:147); guardianship for son John (PLYM COL RECS 3:161); for further information see also NEHGR 111:174, MD 8:203-204, BARNSTABLE FAMS 1:189

THOMAS of Taunton; 1653 inventory sworn by widow Joane Coggen (MD 12:245); in 1661 Jone, wife of Obadiah Miller, was allowed to sell land of deceased husband Thomas Coggen (PLYM COL RECS 4:4-5); for further information see also MA PIONEERS p. 108, NEHGR 111:245

COLBY

JAMES of Rehoboth; 1679 inquest, and guardianship for daughter Elizabeth (PLYM COL RECS 6:8, 13); inventory as John Cobleey (PLYM COL PR 4:1:32)

COLE

JOHN of Plymouth; 1637/8 will, names brother Job Cole executor (MD 2:209, PLYM COL RECS 1:75); settlement (PLYM COL RECS 5:234); for further information see also MA PIONEERS p. 110, TAG 42:120

JOHN of Portsmouth RI; 1676 inventory sworn by widow Mary Cole (PLYM SCRAPBOOK p. 122, PLYM COL PR 3:2:89); doesn't appear to be the same person in RI GEN DICT

COLEMAN

EDWARD, perhaps of Eastham; 1691 Barnstable Co. inventory sworn to by widow Margett Coleman (MD 12:90); for further information see also MA PIONEERS p. 111, TAG 52:137, CAPE COD HIST 2:286, BARNSTABLE FAMS 1:195

JOSEPH Sr. of Scituate; 1674 will names wife Sarah (MD 34:73); for further information see also MA PIONEERS p. 111

COLLAMER

MARY of Scituate; widow of Peter; 1685 inventory (PN&Q 2:99); for further information see also SCITUATE BY DEANE p. 239

COLLAMER con't

PETER Sr. of Scituate; 1683 will, proved 1684, names wife Mary (PLYM COL PR 4:2:142); 1684 inventory (PN&Q 2:99); for further information see also MA PIONEERS p. 111, SCITUATE BY DEANE p. 239, PN&Q 2:99

COLLIER

WILLIAM of Duxbury; 1671 administration granted to Mr. Thomas Prence, and others (PLYM COL RECS 5:68, 80); for further information see also TAG 42:119, 49:215, 51:58, DUXBURY BY WINSOR p. 248, BRIDGEWATER BY MITCHELL p. 385

COMBE/COOMES

DANIEL of Scituate; 1683 will, sworn 1683/4, names Timothy White executor (PLYM COL PR 4:2:68); for further information see also MD 24:135

FRANCIS of Middleboro; grandson of Pilgrim Degory Priest; widow Mary swears to 1682/3 inventory (PLYM COL PR 4:2:52, PLYM SCRAP p. 27); 1683 administration granted to John Richmond and Mrs. Mary Combe (PLYM COL RECS 6:112); for further information see also FAMS OF PILGRIMS (Priest family), GEN ADV 4:31

COOKE

ELIZABETH of Eastham; 1687 Barnstable Co. inventory names husband Josiah Cooke (see Josias below) (MD 4:179); for further information see also TAG 42:198

FRANCIS of Plymouth; came on the ship Mayflower; 1659 will names wife Hester, with inventory exhibited 1663 (MD 2:24 or MAY RDR p. 57); agreement of heirs (MD 3:103); for further information see also FAMS OF PILGRIMS, MD 3:95-105, 8:48, NEHGR 107:61

JACOB Sr. of Plymouth; son of Francis; 1675 will, exhibited 1676, names wife Elizabeth (MD 3:236 or MAY RDR p. 216); settlement (PLYM COL LR 4:108); for further information see also FAMS OF PILGRIMS

JOSIAS/JOSIAH Sr. of Eastham; not a descendant of Pilgrim Francis Cooke; 1673 will names wife Elizabeth, 1687 agreement (MD 4:181, 15:35); administration (PLYM COL RECS 5:132); settlement (PLYM COL RECS 3:37); for further information see also MA PIONEERS p. 115

COOKE con't
THOMAS late of Ipswich; 1650 inquest (PLYM COL RECS 2:151)

COOMES see COMBE

COOPER
JOHN of Barnstable; 1676 will, sworn 1683[/4?], names wife Priscilla (PLYM COL PR 4:2:59, 124); for further information see also MA PIONEERS p. 11, SCITUATE BY DEANE p. 241, BARNSTABLE FAMS 1:192

NATHANIEL of Rehoboth; son of Deacon Thomas Cooper; 1677 inventory and settlement naming wife Judith (PLYM COL PR 3:2:81-82); for further information see also SAVAGE 1:454-5, PLYM COL RECS 6:141

CORNELIUS see MORE

CORNWALL/CORNELL
THOMAS of Portsmouth RI; 1673 settlement names widow Sarah Cornwell and children (PLYM COL RECS 5:133); for further information see also PLYM COL RECS 5:131-132, RI GEN DICT p. 54, RI FAMS 1:255

CORY
WILLIAM of Portsmouth RI; 1681 will, sworn 1681/2, names wife Mary (PLYM COL PR 4:1:106b); for further information see also RI GEN DICT p. 56

COTTERELL
NICHOLAS Sr. of Taunton; 1680 will, sworn 1681, names wife Martha (PLYM COL PR 4:1:97); for further information see also RI GEN DICT (reprint) p. 57, RIGR 5:252

CRISP
GEORGE of Eastham; 1682 will names wife Hephzibay (or Hepzibah) (PLYM COL PR 4:2:14); for further information see also MA PIONEERS p. 122, ASPINWALL RECS pp. 87, 132

CROCKER
JOHN Sr. of Barnstable; 1668/9 will names wife Jone (MD 17:116, 117); 1669 administration (PLYM COL RECS 5:21, 213); for further information see also MA PIONEERS p. 123, BARNSTABLE FAMS 1:200, SCITUATE BY DEANE p. 244

CROCKER con't

SAMUEL of Barnstable; son of William; 1681 trial of man accused of his death (PLYM COL RECS 6:82); for further information see also BARNSTABLE FAMS 1:209

CROW/CROWELL

ELVERTON see YELVERTON

JOHN Sr. of Yarmouth; 1668/9 Barnstable Co. settlement names widow Mehitable Crow (MD 10:101); for further information see also CAPE COD HIST 2:199

THOMAS Sr. of Yarmouth; 1689 inventory sworn by widow Agnes Crowell, 1690 agreement (MD 11:26); for further information see also CAPE COD HIST 2:199, CHATHAM BY SMITH p. 110

WILLIAM of Plymouth; 1683 will names wife Hannah (PLYM COL PR 4:2:54); for further information see also MA PIONEERS p. 125, PLYM ANC LANDMARKS 2:75

WILLIAM, probably of Taunton; 1671 inventory, sworn by Ann Evans, taken in 1670 by Taunton men (PLYM COL RECS 5:276; PLYM SCRAP p. 98)

[Y]ELVERTON of Yarmouth; 1681 will mentions "wife," and names son Thomas executor, 1683/4 inventory (PLYM COL PR 4:2:60); for further information see also NEHGR 125:231, TAG 35:173

CUDWORTH

JAMES of Scituate, Major; 1681 will, 1682 inventory, appoints sons James, Israel and Jonathan executors (PLYM COL PR 4:2:8); for further information see also MA PIONEERS p. 125, SCITUATE BY PRATT p. 210, SCITUATE BY DEANE p. 245

CURTICE

JOHN Sr. of Scituate; 1679 settlement names his eldest brother Thomas Curtice (PLYM COL RECS 6:39); 1680 division (PLYM COL RECS 6:39); 1679/80 bond of administrator Richard Curtis (PLYM SCRAP p. 15); inventory (PLYM COL PR 4:1:52); for further information see also SCITUATE BY DEANE p. 251

CUSHMAN/COACHMAN

JAMES of Scituate; 1648 will names Thomas Lapham executor (MD 9:81); for further information see also MA PIONEERS p. 127

THOMAS Sr. of Plymouth, elder; he married Mary, daughter of Pilgrim Isaac Allerton; 1690 will names wife Mary, 1691 codicil, oath March 1691/2 (MD 4:37 or GEN ADV 2:106-7); for further information see also FAMS OF PILGRIMS (Allerton family), SAVAGE 1:492, BRIDGEWATER BY MITCHELL p. 393

CUTHBERTSON see GODBERTSON

DAGGETT see DOGED

DAMON

JOHN Sr. of Scituate, Sgt.; 1676 administration granted to relict Martha Daman and Arthur Howland, settlement (PLYM COL RECS 5:237, 6:33, 38, 69; PLYM COL PR 3:2:41, 94); for further information see also MA PIONEERS p. 129, SCITUATE BY DEANE p. 260, NGSQ (June 1983); SCITUATE BY PRATT p. 337

JOHN Jr. of Scituate; son of John; 1676 inventory (PLYM COL PR 3:2:42); administration granted to his brother Daniel Damon (PLYM COL RECS 5:213)

DARBEY

JOHN of Yarmouth; 1655 inventory (MD 14:112); 1655/6 oath to inventory by "Widow Darby" (PLYM COL RECS 3:96); settlement (PLYM COL PR 4:2:32); for further information see also MA PIONEERS p. 130, NEHGR 70:438

MATHEW of Barnstable; 1674/5 administration granted to Jabez Lumbart (PLYM COL RECS 5:160); for further information see also NEHGR 70:442

DAVIS

DOLAR of Barnstable; 1672 will names wife Joanna (MD 24:71); 1673 administration (PLYM COL RECS 5:125); for further information see also MA PIONEERS p. 131, BARNSTABLE FAMS 1:289

JOSEPH of Barnstable; 1690 settlement names wife Mary (MD 11:28); for further information see also SAVAGE 2:18, BARNSTABLE FAMS 1:296

NICHOLAS "of Rhode Island, sometimes of Barnstable"; 1673 dower to widow Sarah Davis (PLYM COL RECS 5:124); for further information see also MA PIONEERS p. 133, BARNSTABLE FAMS 1:294, RI GEN DICT p. 63

SIMON; child of Nicholas of Barnstable; 1658 inquest (PLYM COL RECS 3:146); for further information see also BARNSTABLE FAMS 1:296

DAY

WILLIAM; 1660/1 inquest (PLYM COL RECS 3:213)

DEACON

JOHN, no residence given; 1635/6 inquest (PLYM COL RECS 1:39)

DEAN

ALLIS [or Alice] of Taunton; widow of John; 1677 agreement between her heirs and those of her son Lt. Israel Dean (PLYM COL PR 3:2:97); for further information see also MA PIONEERS p. 135

ISRAEL, Lt. of Taunton; son of John; 1677 will names brother Isaac Dean (PLYM COL PR 3:2:96); for further information see also MA PIONEERS p. 135

JOHN of Taunton; 1660 will names wife Alice (MD 17:158); for further information see also MA PIONEERS p. 135

STEVEN, probably of Plymouth; came on the ship Fortune; 1634 inventory (MD 2:87); 1653 oath of Josias Cooke late of Eastham, who married Elizabeth widow of Steven Dean (PLYM COL RECS 3:37); for further information see also TAG 42:198, MA PIONEERS p. 135

DELANO

PHILLIP Sr. of Duxbury; came on the ship Fortune; 1682 settlement of estate mentions unnamed wife (MD 11:250); 1682 bond of administrator Samuel Delano (PLYM COL RECS 6:91); 1681/2 inventory (PLYM SCRAP pp. 29-30); for further information see also MA PIONEERS p. 136, DUXBURY BY WINSOR p. 251, SCITUATE BY DEANE p. 262, TAG 52:91, 53:172

DENNIS

WILLIAM of Scituate; 1649 will, probated 1656, names daughter Judith and her husband William Peakes as executors (MD 14:113); for further information see also MA PIONEERS p. 136, TAG 33:153

DERBY see DARBY

DEXTER

THOMAS of Sandwich; son of Thomas; 1686 Barnstable Co. agreement names widow Elizabeth Dexter (MD 3:176); for further information see also SAVAGE 2:45, ASPINWALL RECS p. 136, CAPE COD HIST 2:78, BARNSTABLE FAMS 1:323

DICKSEY

JOHN of Swansey; 1673 will sworn in 1674 by widow Elizabeth Dicksey (MD 25:120); for further information see also SUFFOLK CO. PROBATE #1663

DILLINGHAM

EDWARD of Sandwich; 1666 will names sons (MD 16:161); 1667 administration granted to Henry and John Dillingham (PLYM COL RECS 4:155); for further information see also MA PIONEERS p. 139, CAPE COD HIST 2:66

DIMACKE/DIMMOCK

THOMAS of Barnstable; 1658 nuncupative will mentions unnamed wife (MD 14:230); for further information see also MA PIONEERS p. 139, BARNSTABLE FAMS 1:328, SCITUATE BY DEANE p. 263

DINGLEY

JACOB of Marshfield; son of John; 1691 administration granted to widow Elizabeth Dingley (MD 31:61 or GEN ADV 2:90); for further information see also MA PIONEERS p. 140, ME HGR 2:120, DUXBURY BY WINSOR p. 255

JOHN of Marshfield; 1689/90 Plymouth Co. settlement names children, but does not mention a wife (GEN ADV 1:75); Plymouth Co. inventory presented by son Jacob Dingley (GEN ADV 1:113 or PN&Q 5:92); for further information see also MA PIONEERS p. 140, DUXBURY BY WINSOR p. 255, TAG 56:207-210 [after publication, author found death date was incorrect]

DIXEY see DICKSEY

DOANE/DONE

Child; 1667 inquest on unnamed child of Daniel of Eastham (PLYM COL RECS 4:169)

JOHN of Eastham; 1678 Barnstable Co. will, sworn 1686, mentions unnamed wife and names son John executor (MD 3:177); for further information see also MA PIONEERS p. 142

DODSON

ANTHONY of Scituate; 1682 agreement between widow Mary Dodson and children (PLYM COL PR 4:1:3); for further information see also SCITUATE BY DEANE p. 263

DOGED/DOGGETT/DAGGETT

JOHN of Plymouth; 1673 will with inventory sworn by widow Bathsheba Doged (MD 25:37, 123, PLYM SCRAP pp. 113-114); for further information see also MA PIONEERS p. 141, MARTHA'S VINEYARD BY BANKS 2:63-66, 3:126

DONE see DOANE

DOTEY/DOTEN

EDWARD Sr. of New Plymouth; came on the ship Mayflower; 1655 will, with surrender of dower rights by widow Faith Dotten (MD 3:87); for further information see also FAMS OF PILGRIMS

EDWARD of Plymouth; son of Edward Sr.; 1689/90 administration granted to widow Sarah Dotey, 1696 agreement of heirs (MD 5:210); Plymouth Co. inventory (GEN ADV 1:113); 1695 Plymouth Co. guardianship (GEN ADV 2:104, 4:88, 92 or MD 31:65); for further information see also FAMS OF PILGRIMS

THOMAS of Plymouth; son of Edward Sr.; 1678 will names wife Mary (MD 4:233, PLYM SCRAP p. 130); inventory dated only 28 Jan., no year (PLYM SCRAP pp. 108-109); for further information see also FAMS OF PILGRIMS, TAG 36:1

DRAYTON

HENRY of Marshfield; 1651 inventory taken by Kenelm Winslow, Josiah Winslow Sr. and John Burne (MD 11:6); 1651/2 administration (PLYM COL RECS 3:4); inquest recorded in 1654/5 (PLYM COL RECS 3:70); for further information see also MA PIONEERS p. 144

DREW

SAMUEL of Plymouth or Duxbury; 1678 inquest (PLYM COL RECS 5:262); for further information see also DUXBURY BY WINSOR p. 256

DUNBAR

JAMES of Bridgewater; 1690 inventory presented by widow Jane Dunbar, 1690/1 settlement (MD 31:15 or GEN ADV 2:61); for further information see also BRIDGEWATER BY MITCHELL p. 149, HINGHAM BY LINCOLN 2:196

DUNHAM

DANIEL of Plymouth; son of John; 1677 will names wife Hannah (PLYM COL PR 3:2:102); for further information see also TAG 30:146

JOHN Sr. of Plymouth; 1669 will names wife Abigail (MD 17:113); administration granted to widow Abigail Dunham Sr. (PLYM COL RECS 5:22); for further information see also TAG 30:144

SAMUEL of Plymouth; son of John; 1687 Plymouth Co. administration granted to his brother John Dunham Jr. (GEN ADV 1:19 or PN&Q 4:107); 1688 inquest (PLYM CO CT RECS 1:193); for further information see also TAG 30:147

DURING

JOHN, residence not given; 1680 inquest (PLYM COL RECS 6:46); perhaps he is the John Durand of Scituate (PLYM COL RECS 8:180)

DWELLEY

SAMUEL of Scituate; son of Richard Sr.; 1690/1 inventory presented by his brother Richard (MD 30:71 or GEN ADV 1:116); for further information see also SCITUATE BY DEANE p. 265

EATON

FRANCIS of Plymouth; came on the ship Mayflower; 1633 inventory which mentions "first wife" (MD 1:197); settlement names widow Christian Eaton (PLYM COL RECS 1:19-20); for further information see also MF 1:1, MQ 41:64

SAMUEL of Middleboro; son of Pilgrim Francis Eaton; married (2) Martha Billington, granddaughter of Pilgrim John Billington; 1684 inventory with settlement (MD 2:172); for further information see also MF 1:5, TG 3:231

WILLIAM of Plymouth; grandson of Pilgrim Francis Eaton; 1690 Plymouth Co. will, mentioning "father and mother," sworn 1690/1 by his father Benjamin Eaton (MD 12:227 or GEN ADV 1:119); for further information see also MF 1:7

ELDRED/ELDRECH

ROBERT of Yarmouth; 1682 division (PLYM COL PR 4:2:25, 26); 1682/3 bond of administrators, widow Elizabeth Eldrich and Nicholas Eldrich (PLYM COL RECS 6:104-105); for further information see also MA PIONEERS p. 153, CHATHAM BY SMITH p. 117

ELLIS

JOHN of Sandwich, Lt.; 1677 inventory sworn by Mistress Elizabeth Ellis, widow (PLYM COL PR 3:2:88); bond of administratrix (PLYM SCRAP p. 127); for further information see also MA PIONEERS p. 155, NEHGR 119:161, LITTLE COMPTON FAMS p. 265

JOHN Jr. of Sandwich; son of Lt. John; 1677 administration (PLYM COL RECS 5:235); 1677 inventory sworn by [his mother] Mistress Elizabeth Ellis, widow (PLYM COL PR 3:2:88); for further information see also NEHGR 119:172

JOSEPH of Scituate; 1676/7 inquest (PLYM COL RECS 5:225)

ENGLAND

JOHN; 1638 inquest (PLYM COL RECS 1:88)

ENGLAND con't
WILLIAM; 1651 inquest on 10 year old servant of Joseph Wilbor of Taunton (PLYM COL RECS 2:175); for further information see also RI GEN DICT p. 72

Englishman; 1658/9 inquest (PLYM COL RECS 3:159)

ENSIGNE
JOHN of Scituate; son of Thomas; 1676 will names his daughter Hannah Ensigne and his mother Elizabeth Ensigne (PLYM COL PR 3:2:16); 1676 appointment of executor (PLYM COL RECS 5:211); for further information see also MD 16:23, SCITUATE BY DEANE p. 267, DUXBURY BY WINSOR p. 257

THOMAS of Scituate; 1663 will names wife Elizabeth (MD 16:22, 23); 1663/4 administration (PLYM COL RECS 4:55); for further information see also MA PIONEERS p. 157, SCITUATE BY DEANE p. 266, TAG 56:219, AMERICAN COLONISTS BY SHERWOOD p. 48, HINGHAM BY LINCOLN 2:213

EVANS/EVANCE
THOMAS, probably of Plymouth; 1634 inventory, taken by John Howland and Jonathan Brewster, mentions unnamed widow (MD 2:88); for further information see also MA PIONEERS p. 158

WILLIAM of Taunton; 1671 inventory sworn by Anna Evance (MD 19:164); for further information see also MA PIONEERS p. 158

EWELL
HENRY of Scituate; 1681 Plymouth Co. will, sworn 1688/9, names wife Sarah (PLYM CO PR 1:273); for further information see also MA PIONEERS p. 159, SCITUATE BY DEANE p. 267, MARSHFIELD BY RICHARDS 2:52

EWER
JOHN, probably of Barnstable; 1652 inventory sworn by widow Mary Ewer (MD 11:10 or PLYM SCRAP p. 12); administration (PLYM COL RECS 3:15)

EWER con't

THOMAS, residence not given; son of Thomas; 1667 inventory sworn by Hannah Ewer, widow (MD 17:24 or PLYM SCRAP p. 63, where he is wrongly called Thomas Huckins); administration (PLYM COL RECS 4:151, 153); for further information see also BARNSTABLE FAMS 1:360

FALLOWELL

GABRIEL of Plymouth; 1667 will names wife Katheren (MD 17:25); for further information see also MA PIONEERS p. 160

JOHN of Plymouth; son of William; 1675 inventory sworn by widow Sarah Fallowell (PLYM COL PR 3:1:54); 1675 inquest and administrator appointed (PLYM COL RECS 5:182, 188); for further information see also MA PIONEERS p. 160

JONATHAN; son of William and grandson of Gabriel; Jonathan's undated will [recorded on the same page as the 1676 inventory of Peter Hunt] names brothers John and Samuel (PLYM COL PR 3:2:45); 1676 administration (PLYM COL RECS 5:213); for further information see also MA PIONEERS p. 160, MD 1:132, 17:25

KATHEREN of Plymouth; 1673 will, exhibited 1676, names deceased husband Gabriel (PLYM COL PR 3:2:43); administration (PLYM COL RECS 5:204); for further information see also MA PIONEERS p. 160

FAUNCE

JOHN Sr. of Plymouth; came on the ship Anne; 1653 inventory sworn by widow Patience Faunce (MD 11:159); 1653/4 administration (PLYM COL RECS 3:46); in 1668 Thomas Faunce was acknowledged as his heir apparent (PLYM COL RECS 5:6); for further information see also NEHGR 114:115, 116:188

FINNEY

ROBERT Sr. of Plymouth; 1686 Suffolk Co. will, sworn 1687, names wife Phebe (SUFFOLK CO. PROBATE #1624); for further information see also MA PIONEERS p. 166

ROBERT of Plymouth; 1690 Plymouth Co. will names brother Josiah executor (MD 30:139, 140, GEN ADV 1:118-119); for further information see also BARNSTABLE FAMS 2:226

FISH

AMBROS of Sandwich; 1691 Barnstable Co. inventory and settlement names widow Hannah Fish (MD 12:89); for further information see also TAG 35:42

FISH con't

JOHN of Sandwich; 1663 inventory sworn by widow Syselia [or Cecelia] Fish (MD 16:22 or PLYM SCRAP pp. 30-31); 1664 administration (PLYM COL RECS 4:58); for further information see also MA PIONEERS p. 166

THOMAS; son of Nathaniel of Sandwich; 1664/5 inquest (PLYM COL RECS 4:84-85)

FOBES

JOHN of Bridgewater; undated will, recorded with 1661 documents, mentions unnamed wife (MD 15:59); inventory sworn in 1663 by "Constant Briggs sometimes the wife of the said John Fobes" (MD 15:60); for further information see also PLYM COL MARR p. 17, MA PIONEERS p. 171, LITTLE COMPTON FAMS p. 271, BRIDGEWATER BY MITCHELL p. 162, DUXBURY BY WINSOR p. 258

FOLLAND

THOMAS Sr. of Yarmouth; 1686 Barnstable Co. will names son Thomas (MD 3:176); for further information see also TAG 48:6, YARMOUTH BY SWIFT p. 75 (Falland family), MA PIONEERS p. 235 under Holland [the will shows that the double lower case "f" used to begin the name can easily be misread as "H"]

FORD

JOSEPH of Bristol [now RI]; 1690/1 administration to widow Deborah Ford, with inventory (SUFFOLK CO. PROBATE #1864); for further information see also EARLY REHOBOTH 1:73

WILLIAM Sr. of Marshfield; 1676 will, with inventory sworn by widow Anne Ford (PLYM COL PR 3:2:22-23); for further information see also MA PIONEERS p. 172, DUXBURY BY WINSOR p. 259, MARSHFIELD BY RICHARDS 2:102

FORSTER

JAMES, late of London, Capt.; 1685/6 Barnstable Co. will names his mother Elizabeth, wife of Mr. John Torlton (MD 2:176)

FOSTER

BENJAMIN, of Sandwich, Sgt.; descendant of Pilgrim Richard Warren; 1690 Barnstable Co. inventory sworn by Jonathan Morey Jr. (MD 11:28); for further information see also TAG 32:193

EDWARD of Barnstable; 1643 will, sworn 1644, names wife Lettice (MD 6:248); 1644 oaths authorized (PLYM COL RECS 2:73, 75); for further information see also MA PIONEERS p. 172

JAMES see FORSTER, JAMES

RICHARD of Plymouth; married Mary Bartlett, granddaughter of Pilgrim Richard Warren; 1659 agreement names widow Mary Foster (MD 14:15); for further information see also FAMS OF PILGRIMS (Warren family), TAG 32:193

FOXWELL

RICHARD of Barnstable; 1668 will names sons[-in-law] Hugh Cole and Samuel Bacon executors (MD 17:28); 1668 administration (PLYM COL RECS 4:192); inventory (PLYM SCRAP pp. 59-60); bond of administrators (PLYM SCRAP p. 72); for further information see also MA PIONEERS p. 174, BARNSTABLE FAMS p. 366, SCITUATE BY DEANE p. 272

FREEMAN

EDMOND Sr. of Sandwich; 1682 will names as executors daughter Elizabeth Ellis and his "sons" Edmond Freeman, John Freeman and Edward Perrey (MD 12:248); for further information see also MA PIONEERS p. 175, TAG 40:104, CAPE COD HIST 2:36, BARNSTABLE FAMS p. 385

WILLIAM of Eastham; son of John; 1687 Barnstable Co. inventory was presented by widow Lydia Freeman (MD 3:177); settlement (MD 13:19, 31:35); for further information see also CAPE COD HIST 2:757

FRENCH

RICHARD of Marshfield; 1688 Plymouth Co. administration granted to his widow Martha French (GEN ADV 1:42 or PN&Q 5:15); for further information see also SAVAGE 2:207, CAMBRIDGE BY PAIGE p. 551

FULLER

JOHN of Rehoboth; not a Mayflower line; 1676 settlement mentions but does not name widow who is to be assisted by her unnamed father and father-in-law (PLYM COL RECS 5:212); inventory names widow Abigail Fuller (PLYM COL PR 3:2:70); for further information see also SAVAGE 2:216

JOHN of Barnstable, Dr.; son of Matthew; 1691 Barnstable Co. inventory names widow Hannah Fuller (MD 12:187); 1700 receipts name administratrix Hannah Lothrop alias Fuller (MD 33:171); for further information see also FAMS OF PILGRIMS (Edward Fuller family), BARNSTABLE FAMS p. 382

MATTHEW, of Barnstable, Capt.; presumed to be son of Edward of the ship Mayflower; 1678 will names wife Frances (MD 13:7); action re property (PLYM COL RECS 5:272); for further information see also NEHGR 55:192-195, 410-416 and FAMS OF PILGRIMS (Edward Fuller family), BARNSTABLE FAMS p. 376

SAMUEL, elder of Plymouth; came on the ship Mayflower; 1633 will mentions unnamed wife, and names young son Samuel executor (MD 1:24, 2:8 or MQ 37:2:55); will proved (PLYM COL RECS 1:18); for further information see also MQ 41:99, FAMS OF PILGRIMS (Samuel Fuller family), MF 1:49

SAMUEL of Barnstable, Lt.; son of Matthew; 1675 will, sworn 1676, names wife Mary (PLYM COL PR 3:1:179-180); for further information see also FAMS OF PILGRIMS (Edward Fuller family), BARNSTABLE FAMS p. 381

SAMUEL Sr. of Barnstable; son of Pilgrim Edward Fuller; came on the ship Mayflower; 1683 will names sons Samuel and John Fuller executors (MD 2:237); for further information see also FAMS OF PILGRIMS (Edward Fuller family)

SAMUEL of Barnstable; son of Samuel and grandson of Pilgrim Edward Fuller; 1691 Barnstable Co. inventory and quitclaim by sons mentions "their deceased mother" (MD 12:189); for further information see also NEHGR 9:281, MD 2:238-239, 13:8, FAMS OF PILGRIMS (Edward Fuller family)

FULLER con't

SAMUEL of Rehoboth; son of Robert; not a <u>Mayflower</u> line; 1676 inventory sworn by widow Mary Fuller (PLYM COL PR 3:2:47); 1677 administration (PLYM COL RECS 5:234, 237); for further information see also SAVAGE 2:219

GANNETT/GANNATT

BENJAMIN of Scituate; son of Mathew; 1690/1 Plymouth Co. administration granted to his brother Joseph Gannett (MD 30:69 or GEN ADV 1:116); bond of administrator (PLYM SCRAP p. 73); for further information see also SCITUATE BY DEANE p. 273

THOMAS of Bridgewater; 1655 will, with inventory sworn by widow Sarah Gannett (MD 7:38); administration (PLYM COL RECS 3:88); for further information see also MA PIONEERS p. 181, BRIDGEWATER BY MITCHELL p. 169

GARDINER

SAMUEL of Plymouth; 1689/90 inventory sworn by widow Susanna Gardiner, with settlement (PN&Q 5:108 or GEN ADV 1:113 or PLYM CO CT RECS 1:210); guardianships (GEN ADV 2:104, 4:88); for further information see also PLYM ANC LANDMARKS 2:116

GARRETT

RICHARD of Scituate; 1662 Suffolk Co. inventory, sworn by widow Lydia Garrett on July 29, says he died 29 March 1662 (SUFFOLK CO PROBATE OLD SERIES 4:94); for further information see also TAG 38:74, PLYM COL RECS 4:44, SCITUATE BY DEANE p. 274

GIFFORD

WILLIAM of Sandwich; 1687 will names wife Mary (MD 3:202); for further information see also NEHGR 128:241, LITTLE COMPTON FAMS p. 276

GILBERT

JOHN Sr. of Taunton; 1654 will, probated 1657, names wife Winnifred (MD 14:114); for further information see also MA PIONEERS p. 186, TAG 27:9, NEHGR 111:234, NGSQ 69:40

THOMAS Sr. of Taunton; son of John; 1677 administration granted to widow Jane Gilbert and son Thomas Gilbert (PLYM COL PR 3:2:78); settlement (PLYM COL PR 3:2:101); for further information see also MA PIONEERS p. 186, PLYM COL MAR p. 18, PLYM COL RECS 5:232-233, NEHGR 111:234, NGSQ 69:40

GILPIN

ANTHONY of Barnstable; 1655 will names kinsman William Hodgis and others in England (MD 14:21); administration granted to Nathaniel Bacon (PLYM COL RECS 3:83); for further information see also MA PIONEERS p. 188, BARNSTABLE FAMS 1:406

GILSON

WILLIAM of Scituate; 1639 will, with codicil, names wife Francis (MD 3:160); estate to be proved (PLYM COL RECS 1:141); for further information see also MA PIONEERS p. 188, PLYM COL RECS 2:140-143, SCITUATE BY DEANE p. 275

GLASS

JAMES of Plymouth; 1652 inventory sworn by widow Mary Glass (MD 11:94); inquest (PLYM COL RECS 3:16); for further information see also MA PIONEERS p. 188, NEHGR 111:178, DUXBURY BY WINSOR p. 262

JAMES of Duxbury; son of Roger; 1690 Plymouth Co. will, sworn 1691, names brother John Glass (MD 31:17 or GEN ADV 2:62); for further information see also DUXBURY BY WINSOR p. 262, NEHGR 111:178

GLOVER

JOSSE/JOSEPH, Rev., of Sutton in Surrey, England; 1640 debt settlement by widow Elizabeth Glover, executrix of the estate (PLYM COL RECS 1:151); for further information see also CAMBRIDGE BY PAIGE p. 559, NEHGR 30:26-28

GODBERTSON

GODBERT & wife SARAH of Plymouth; she widow of Pilgrim Degory Priest and sister of Pilgrim Isaac Allerton; Godbert and Sarah came on the ship ANNE; 1633 joint inventory (MD 1:154); for further information see also MA PIONEERS p. 189, PLYM COL RECS 1:18-20, 25, 2:119

GODFREY/GODFREE

FRANCIS of Bridgewater; 1666 will, exhibited 1669, names wife Elizabeth (MD 17:155); for further information see also MA PIONEERS p. 189

RICHARD Sr. of Taunton; 1691 Bristol Co. will names wife Mary (GEN ADV 4:125); for further information see also NEHGR 123:34, 230

GOODSPEED

ALICE Sr. of Barnstable; widow of Roger; 1688 Barnstable Co. will, proved 1689, names son Ebenezer executor (MD 10:102); for further information see also BARNSTABLE FAMS 1:391, MA PIONEERS p. 192

BENJAMIN of Barnstable; son of Roger; 1677 will names wife Mary (PLYM COL PR 3:2:94-95); for further information see also MA PIONEERS p. 192, BARNSTABLE FAMS 1:399

NATHANIEL of Barnstable; son of Roger; 1670 administration granted to widow Elizabeth Goodspeed (PLYM COL RECS 5:42-43); inventory (MD 18:251 or PLYM SCRAP p. 88); for further information see also MA PIONEERS p. 192, BARNSTABLE FAMS 1:398

ROGER of Barnstable; 1685 will names wife Alice (PLYM COL LR 5:329-330); witnesses sworn 1685 (PLYM COL RECS 6:170); for further information see also BARNSTABLE FAMS 1:391

GORHAM/GORUM etc.

DESIRE of Yarmouth; wife of John Gorham, and daughter of Pilgrim John Howland; 1683 inventory (MD 4:217); settlement names son James (MD 4:217 or PLYM COL RECS 6:124); guardians chosen (PLYM COL RECS 6:125); for further information see also FAMS OF PILGRIMS (Howland family)

JOHN of Yarmouth, Capt.; married Desire Howland, daughter of Pilgrim John Howland; 1675 administration granted to widow Desire Gorham, James Gorham and John Gorham (MD 4:153, PLYM COL RECS 5:188); children's portions (PLYM COL RECS 5:187); bond of administrators (PLYM SCRAP p. 120); for further information see also MA PIONEERS p. 194, YARMOUTH BY SWIFT p. 61, MD 4:28, 17:251, CAPE COD HIST 2:273, FAMS OF PILGRIMS (Howland family), BARNSTABLE FAMS 1:407

GOULD

MARY of Taunton; daughter of John; 1678 inquest (PLYM COL RECS 5:273); for further information see also SAVAGE 2:285

GRANGER

GRACE of Scituate; 1648 will names son John (MD 9:85); for further information see also MA PIONEERS p. 196, SCITUATE BY DEANE p. 275

JOHN of Marshfield; probably son of Thomas of Scituate; 1656 inventory (MD 14:23); administration granted to Richard Beare (PLYM COL RECS 3:97-98); for further information see also MA PIONEERS p. 196

THOMAS of Scituate; 1642 administration granted to Timothy Hatherly and Edward Eddenton mentions Granger's wife and children but does not name them (PLYM COL RECS 2:50); for further information see also PLYM COL RECS 2:44

GRAY

EDWARD of Plymouth; his first wife was a granddaughter of Pilgrim James Chilton; 1681 adminstration to widow Dorothy Gray (PLYM COL RECS 6:65-66); guardians chosen (ibid. 6:141); dower to widow (ibid. 6:103); widow's consent to division (ibid. 6:147); account (ibid. 6:149); estate settled and dower (PLYM COL LR 4:180, 5:180, 210-211, 223, 229, 230, 287, 301 and many other references in PLYM COL RECS); for further information see also MF 2:15, FAMS OF PILGRIMS (Chilton family), PLYM SCRAP pp. 16-17, RI GEN DICT p. 85

JOHN of Yarmouth; 1673 inventory sworn by widow Hannah Gray (MD 25:122); estate (PLYM COL RECS 5:139); for further information see also MA PIONEERS p. 198

GREAT HARRY see HARRY

GREEN

HENRY of Taunton; 1676 inventory (PLYM COL PR 3:2:18); administration granted to Samuel Hall (PLYM COL RECS 5:213); 1678/9 bond of administrator (PLYM COL RECS 6:6)

JOHN of Sandwich; 1659 will, exhibited 1660, mentions unnamed sister and her child, and names James Skiffe Sr. executor (MD 17:157); for further information see also MA PIONEERS p. 198

HACKE

WILLIAM of Taunton; 1667 administration on estate of William Hacke, who had departed for England several years earlier, was granted to wife Mary Hack (PLYM COL RECS 4:151, 155-6); inventory mentions wife Mary and her child (MD 17:22); for further information see also SAVAGE 2:326

HALL

EDWARD of Rehoboth; November 1671 [sic] will, sworn July 1671, names wife Esther, with inventory 6 March 1670 (MD 19:62); bond of administratrix (PLYM SCRAP pp. 95, 96); for further information see also MA PIONEERS p. 207

GEORGE of Taunton; 1669 will mentions unnamed wife, 1669/70 inventory sworn by widow Mary Hall (MD 18:250); for further information see also MA PIONEERS p. 207

SAMUEL Sr. of Taunton; 1688/9 will, sworn 1690, names wife Elizabeth (GEN ADV 3:122); for further information see also SAVAGE 2:338

HALLETT/HOLLETT

ANDREW of Yarmouth; not a son of Andrew Sr.; 1681/2 will, proved 1684, names wife Ann (PLYM COL PR 4:2:134); for further information see also MA PIONEERS p. 209, TAG 37:84-85, YARMOUTH BY SWIFT p. 53, BARNSTABLE FAMS 1:482

JOHN of Scituate; 1669 will names wife Anne, 1674 inventory (MD 34:113); 1675 bond of administrator (PLYM SCRAP p. 121); for further information see also SCITUATE BY DEANE p. 277

SAMUEL of Barnstable; 1650 adminstration granted to Thomas Howes and Samuel Mayo (PLYM COL RECS 2:156); for further information see also BARNSTABLE FAMS 1:480

HALLOWAY/HALLOWELL see HOLLOWAY

HAMLIN/HAMBLEN

JAMES Sr. of Barnstable; 1683 Barnstable Co. will names wife Anne, 1690 inventory (MD 12:38); for further information see also BARNSTABLE FAMS 1:522

HAMPTON

THOMAS of Sandwich; 1637 will, sworn 1638, makes bequests to many people, none called kin, and names Thomas Tupper and others as executors (MD 3:74; PLYM COL RECS 1:97, 118); for further information see also MA PIONEERS p. 210

HANMER/HANDMORE

JOHN Sr. of Scituate; 1676 will, sworn 1676/7, names wife Hannah (PLYM COL PR 3:2:56); administration granted to John Jr. (PLYM COL RECS 5:220); for further information see also SCITUATE BY DEANE p. 278

JOSEPH of Scituate; 1691 Plymouth Co. bond of administrator Nathaniel Thomas (PLYM CO PR #9117); administration probably of this Joseph (PLYM CO CT RECS 1:210)

HARDING

MARTHA, probably of Plymouth; 1633 account mentions unnamed son (MD 1:82); administration granted to John Done (PLYM COL RECS 1:18); for further information see also MA PIONEERS p. 212

HARLOW

WILLIAM Sr. of Plymouth, Sgt.; married Rebecca Bartlett, granddaughter of Pilgrim Richard Warren; 1691 settlement, administration granted to widow Mary Harlow (MD 12:195 or GEN ADV 2:89); for further information see also FAMS OF PILGRIMS (Warren family), MA PIONEERS p. 213

HARMER

EPHRAIM of Rehoboth; 1683/4 administration granted to Jonathan Bliss (PLYM COL RECS 6:121); for further information see also SAVAGE 2:357, EARLY REHOBOTH 4:33 footnote

HARRIS

ARTHUR of Boston; 1673 will, sworn 1674, mentions unnamed wife and eldest son Isaac (SUFFOLK CO PROBATE OLD SERIES 6:48); 1679 agreement between widow Martha Harris and son Isaac Harris (PLYM COL RECS 6:12); for further information see also MA PIONEERS p. 214, BRIDGEWATER BY MITCHELL pp. 175-176

HARRY

GREAT, an Indian killed by his wife Betty; 1684/5 inquest (PLYM COL RECS 6:153)

HARVEY

JONATHAN of Taunton; 1691 agreement on estate of William Harvey mentions that Jonathan is also deceased (GEN ADV 4:60-1)

WILLIAM of Taunton; 1691 Bristol Co. will and agreement names son Jonathan executor (GEN ADV 4:60-1)

HATCH

THOMAS of Barnstable; wife Grace deposed to 1661 inventory (MD 17:160); 1662/3 administration granted to Jonathan Hatch and Lydia Taylor, wife of Henry (PLYM COL RECS 4:31); for further information see also BARNSTABLE FAMS 1:461

Child; 1680 inquest on unnamed child of Thomas of Scituate (PLYM COL RECS 6:45)

THOMAS of Scituate; 1684 administration (PLYM COL RECS 6:147); 1684 inventory, 1686 settlement names widow Sarah Hatch (PLYM COL PR 4:2:152-3); bond of administratrix (PLYM SCRAP p. 57); for further information see also SCITUATE BY DEANE p. 280 [very confused account in MA PIONEERS p. 219 should not be accepted as fact], NEHGR 70:258, 75:225

WILLIAM the elder of Scituate; 1651 will, exhibited 1652, names wife Jane (MD 10:38); for further information see also MA PIONEERS p. 219, SCITUATE BY DEANE p. 279, NEHGR 70:258

WILLIAM Jr. of Scituate; 1653 will, probated 1657, names wife Abigail (MD 14:114); administration (PLYM COL RECS 3:114); for further information see also NEHGR 70:258

HATHERLEY

TIMOTHY of Scituate; came on the ship Anne; 1664 will, exhibited 1666, names wife Lydia (MD 16:158, 163); administration (PLYM COL RECS 4:138, 155, 5:140); for further information see also SCITUATE BY DEANE p. 280, SCITUATE BY PRATT p. 284

HAWARD/HAYWARD/HOWARD etc.

JAMES of Bridgewater; son of John Howard; 1690/1 inventory sworn by widow Elizabeth Haward (MD 30:187 or GEN ADV 2:61); for further information see also BRIDGEWATER BY MITCHELL p. 198

THOMAS Sr. of Bridgewater; 1678 will, inventory 1680/1, names son Joseph executor (PLYM COL PR 4:1:84, 86); for further information see also BRIDGEWATER BY MITCHELL p. 181

HAYMAN

NATHAN of Bristol [now RI], Capt.; 1689 Bristol Co. inventory sworn by his widow Elizabeth, now wife of Nathaniel Blagrove (BRISTOL CO PR 1:147 or NEHGR 63:129); account, receipts and division (BRISTOL CO PR 2:47, 74A, 176); for further information see also CHARLESTOWN BY WYMAN p. 489, SAVAGE 2:388

HAZELL

JOHN of Seekonk; his 1651 will does not mention wife or family, but bequeaths to William Devell (MD 10:200); MA PIONEERS p. 218, MD 13:39-40

HEDGE/HEDGIS

WILLIAM of Taunton; 1654 inventory sworn by widow Mary (MD 12:246); for further information see also NEHGR 111:319, MA PIONEERS p. 226

WILLIAM Sr. of Yarmouth, Capt.; 1670 will names wife Blanch (MD 18:252); administration granted to Elisha Hedge (PLYM COL RECS 5:43, 47); 1673 guardianship of daughter (PLYM COL RECS 5:124); for further information see also NEHGR 111:319, YARMOUTH BY SWIFT p. 67

HEYLAND see HYLAND

HEWES

JOHN of Scituate; 1671 will, sworn 1674, names wife Joanna (MD 34:112); SCITUATE BY DEANE p. 283

HEWET

MARTHA of Marshfield; 1691 will names deceased husband John Hewet and deceased father Christopher Winter (MD 31:63 or GEN ADV 2:91); for further information see also SAVAGE 2:490, MARSHFIELD VR p. 10

HICKS/HIX

EPHRAIM, of Plymouth; son of Robert below; 1649 inventory (MD 9:226); bond of widow Margaret as administratrix (PLYM SCRAP p. 10); administration (PLYM COL RECS 2:148); in 1660 the court allowed his estate to be used for his aged mother Margaret Hickes (PLYM COL RECS 3:202-203, 217-218); for further information see also PLYM COL RECS 8:8, TAG 51:58

MARGARET; widow of Robert below; came on the ship Anne; 1665 will names son-in-law George Watson one of her executors (MD 16:157); 1665/6 administration (PLYM COL RECS 4:117); for further information see also TAG 51:57

ROBERT of Plymouth; came on the ship Fortune; 1645 will names wife Margaret, 1647 inventory (MD 8:143); for further information see also TAG 51:57, 54:31, MA PIONEERS p. 232 [LITTLE COMPTON FAMS badly confuses this family], DUXBURY BY WINSOR p. 266

SAMUEL of Dartmouth; came on the ship Anne; 1677 inventory sworn by widow Lydia (PLYM COL PR 3:2:89); for further information see also TAG 51:57, LITTLE COMPTON FAMS p. 339, BARNSTABLE FAMS 2:72

THOMAS of Scituate; 1652 will, sworn 1653, names wife Margaret (MD 11:160, PLYM COL RECS 3:37); for further information see also MA PIONEERS p. 232, SCITUATE BY DEANE p. 283

HIGGINS

BENJAMIN of Eastham; 1691 Barnstable Co. inventory and settlement names wife Lydia Higgins (MD 12:89); for further information see also MD 8:12, SAVAGE 2:411

HILAND see HYLAND

HINCKLEY

SAMUEL Sr. of Barnstable; 1662 will names wife Bridgett (MD 12:203); 1663 oath of Samuel Hinckley to will (PLYM COL RECS 4:36); for further information see also MA PIONEERS p. 231, SCITUATE BY DEANE p. 284, BARNSTABLE FAMS 2:30

HINCKLEY con't

THOMAS Jr. of Barnstable; son of Thomas; 1688 Barnstable Co. will names parents Thomas and Mary (MD 10:6); for further information see also BARNSTABLE FAMS 2:35

HINTON

JOHN of Bristol [then in Massachusetts, now in Rhode Island]; 1687 Bristol Co. will names as his heir, Susanna Gladding, daughter of John (GEN ADV 3:118)

HIX see HICKS

HOAR see HORE

HOCKING

JOHN, probably of Maine; 1634 testimony re his death in an incident on Kennebec River [now in Maine] (MD 2:10-11); for further information see also SAVAGE 2:438, WINTHROP'S JNL 1:123-124, 128-129, 131, 137, MASS BAY RECS 1:119

HODGIS see MILLER

HOLLAND see FOLLAND

HOLLETT see HALLETT

HOLLEY see also HOLLOWAY

JOSEPH Sr., probably of Sandwich; 1665 release of son Joseph Jr. (PLYM COL RECS 4:87-88); for further information see also MA PIONEERS p. 236

HOLLOWAY/HOLWAY/HOLLOWELL

ELISHA of Taunton; 1679 inventory sworn by Mary Hollowey (PLYM COL PR 4:1:31); for further information see also MA PIONEERS p. 236 (under William)

JOSEPH of Sandwich; 1647 inventory sworn by widow Rose Holway (MD 8:207); for further information see also MA PIONEERS p. 236

HOLLOWAY/HOLWAY/HOLLOWELL con't

WILLIAM of Marshfield; 1653 inventory (MD 11:158 or PLYM SCRAP p. 96); 1652/3 administration granted to widow Grace Hallowell (PLYM COL RECS 3:22); 1653/4 settlement (PLYM COL RECS 3:45); 1666 portion to daughter (PLYM COL RECS 4:136); for further information see also MA PIONEERS p. 236

HOLMES

ISRAEL of Marshfield; married Desire, daughter of Pilgrim Edward Doty; 1684/5 inquest (PLYM COL RECS 6:147); 1685 inventory sworn by widow Desire Holmes (MD 4:173); 1701 guardianship (GEN ADV 3:27); for further information see also SAVAGE 2:452, FAMS OF PILGRIMS (Doty family)

JOHN of Duxbury; 1675 will, exhibited 1675/6, names wife Mary (PLYM COL PR 3:1:169); for further information see also SAVAGE 2:452, DUXBURY BY WINSOR p. 178

SAMUEL of Marshfield; 1690/1 inventory sworn by widow Mary Holmes (MD 30:142 or GEN ADV 2:26); for further information see also SAVAGE 2:454

WILLIAM died at Boston, Major; 1649 will names sister-in-law Margaret Webb alias Holmes and deceased brother Thomas Holmes (MD 14:153); bond of Job Hawkins (PLYM SCRAP p. 14); for further information see also MA PIONEERS p. 238

WILLIAM of Marshfield; 1677/8 will names sons Israel and Isaac executors and mentions unnamed "beloved wife" (PLYM COL PR 4:1:2c-3c); for further information see also SCITUATE BY DEANE p. 287

HOLWAY see HOLLOWAY

HOPKINS

ELIZABETH; unmarried daughter of Stephen Hopkins below; 1659 inventory indicates that she was then missing and presumed dead (MD 4:118); for further information see also NEHGR 102:48

HOPKINS con't

GILES of Eastham; came on the ship Mayflower with father Stephen; 1682 will with 1688/9 codicil, probated 1690, mentions wife "Catorne" [Catherine] (MD 1:110); for further information see also FAMS OF PILGRIMS, NEHGR 102:48

STEPHEN of Plymouth; came on the ship Mayflower; 1644 will mentions unnamed "deceased wife" and names son Caleb executor (MD 2:12 or MQ 27:4:7); will proved (PLYM COL RECS 2:75); daughters's portions (MD 4:114); for further information see also FAMS OF PILGRIMS, NEHGR 102:46, TAG 39:95, 170, MD 5:47, MQ 35:52

HORE

ELIZABETH of Yarmouth, widow; 1680 will appoints John Rider executor (MD 15:64)

HOUSE see HOWES

HOWARD see HAWARD

HOWELL

THOMAS of Marshfield; 1647 will names Job Lanne executor and mentions unnamed wife (MD 8:87, 209); administration (PLYM COL RECS 2:126-7); 1651/2 account (PLYM COL RECS 3:3, 11, 14); for further information see also MA PIONEERS p. 243, PLYM COL RECS 12:175

HOWES/HOUSE/HOWSE

SAMUEL Sr. of Scituate; 1661 inventory mentions unnamed wife and son Samuel (MD 15:59); administration granted to son and daughter Samuel House Jr. and Elizabeth House (PLYM COL RECS 4:5); 1663 account requested (PLYM COL RECS 4:45); 1663 bond of children's guardians (PLYM SCRAP pp. 19-20); for further information see also MA PIONEERS p. 242, BARNSTABLE FAMS 2:54, SCITUATE BY DEANE p. 289, ASPINWALL RECS p. 224

SARAH of Yarmouth; 1682/3 will mentions deceased husband Capt. Thomas Howes (MD 6:163); for further information see also SAVAGE 2:478

HOWES/HOUSE/HOWSE con't

THOMAS of Yarmouth; 1665 will names wife Mary (MD 6:157); 1665/6 administration granted to widow (PLYM COL RECS 4:117); for further information see also SAVAGE 2:478, YARMOUTH BY SWIFT p. 49

THOMAS of Yarmouth, Capt.; 1675/6 will names wife Sarah (MD 6:160); son choses guardian (PLYM COL RECS 6:134); for further information see also SAVAGE 2:478

WILLIAM of Sandwich; 1663/4 inquest (PLYM COL RECS 4:49-50)

HOWLAND

ARTHUR of Marshfield; brother of Pilgrim John Howland; 1674/5 will, exhibited 1675, names wife Margaret (PLYM COL PR 3:1:160); for further information see also NEHGR 104:221, MA PIONEERS p. 243, DUXBURY BY WINSOR p. 270, TAG 14:214-215, NGSQ (June 1983)

BETHIA Jr. of Plymouth; daughter of Jabez and granddaughter of Pilgrim John Howland; 1676 inquest (PLYM COL RECS 5:208); for further information see also FAMS OF PILGRIMS

ELIZABETH of Swansea; widow of John Howland and daughter of John Tilley, both of whom came on the ship *Mayflower*; came on the ship *Mayflower* herself; 1686 Bristol Co. will names her son-in-law James Browne and son Jabez Howland executors (MD 3:54 or GEN ADV 3:119); for further information see also FAMS OF PILGRIMS, TAG 52:198

HENRY of Duxbury; brother of Pilgrim John Howland; 1670 will names wife Mary (MD 19:32); for further information see also NEHGR 104:221, DUXBURY BY WINSOR p. 270, LITTLE COMPTON FAMS p. 353, NGSQ (forthcoming)

JOHN of Plymouth; came on the ship *Mayflower*; 1672 will, exhibited 1672/3, names wife Elizabeth Howland (MD 2:70); 1672/3 administration PLYM COL RECS 5:110); bond of administratrix (MD 13:65); for further information see also FAMS OF PILGRIMS, NEHGR 104:221, BARNSTABLE FAMS 2:49, DUXBURY BY WINSOR p. 269, SCITUATE BY DEANE p. 400

HOWLAND con't

JOHN of Freetown; son of Henry; 1687 administration granted to brother Samuel Howland (GEN ADV 3:118); for further information see also NGSQ (forthcoming)

MARGARET of Marshfield; 1683 will, sworn 1683/4, names deceased husband Arthur Howland (PLYM COL PR 4:2:122-123); for further information see also DUXBURY BY WINSOR p. 270, NGSQ (June 1983)

MARY of Duxbury; 1674 will, probated 1675, names deceased husband Henry (PLYM COL PR 3:2:10); for further information see also DUXBURY BY WINSOR p. 270, NGSQ (forthcoming)

ZOETH (or ZOAR) of Dartmouth; 1677 inventory sworn by widow Abigail Howland (PLYM COL PR 3:2:84); 1678 settlement (PLYM COL PR 3:2:120);for further information see also LITTLE COMPTON FAMS p. 353, NGSQ (forthcoming)

HOWSE see HOWES

HUCKENS/HUCKINGS

JOHN of Barnstable; 1678/9 settlement names his widow Hope (MD 24:180); 1678 inventory (PLYM COL PR 4:1:8); for further information see also BARNSTABLE FAMS 2:65

THOMAS Sr. of Barnstable; 1679/80 settlement names widow Rose Huckins (MD 24:181); for further information see also MA PIONEERS p. 246, BARNSTABLE FAMS 2:58 (Note: the inventory in PLYM SCRAP p. 63, listed as that of Thomas Huckins, is actually that of Thomas Ewer.)

HUDSON

JOHN of Duxbury; 1683 Plymouth Co. will, proved 1688, names wife Ann (GEN ADV 1:42 or PN&Q 5:13); for further information see also DUXBURY BY WINSOR p. 271

HUETT see HEWET

HULL

TRISTRUM of Barnstable; son of Rev. Joseph Hull; 1666 will and codicil, sworn 1666/7, names wife Blanch (MD 17:23); 1666/7 administration (PLYM COL RECS 4:141); 1667/8 children's guardians appointed (PLYM COL RECS 4:175, 5:52); for further information see also BARNSTABLE FAMS 2:28, MA PIONEERS (under Rev. Joseph)

HUNT

EDWARD of Duxbury; 1656 inventory, taken by Christopher Wadsworth and Constant Southworth, does not mention any wife or family (MD 14:227); for further information see also MA PIONEERS p. 248, DUXBURY RECS p. 7, PLYM COL RECS 3:302, BRIDGEWATER BY MITCHELL p. 401 (wrongly listed under Edmund Hunt)

PETER Jr.; 1676 inventory taken at Rehoboth, sworn by widow Rebecca (PLYM COL PR 3:45, 3:2:51); 1677 administration (PLYM COL RECS 5:234, 237); 1677 settlement of estate (PLYM COL PR 3:2:109)

THOMAS of Duxbury; 1676/7 inventory includes part of unnamed father's estate (PLYM COL PR 3:2:84); administration granted to Samuel Hunt (PLYM COL RECS 5:220); for further information see also SAVAGE 2:501

HUNTER

THOMAS of Titicut, Indian; 1685 will names wife Hannah (PLYM COL LR 5:347); for further information see also PLYM COL RECS 12:243

HURST

GARTHEREW [or Gertrude]; widow of James; 1670 inventory sworn by John Cobb who referred to her as "Grandmother Hurst" (MD 18:251); 1688 list of debts (PLYM SCRAP pp. 68, 90-91) for further information see also MA PIONEERS p. 249

JAMES of Plymouth; 1657 will, proved 1657/8, names wife Garteud [or Gertrude] (MD 14:228); for further information see also MA PIONEERS p. 249

WILLIAM of Sandwich; 1641 administration granted to widow Katherine Hurst (PLYM COL RECS 2:18); for further information see also MA PIONEERS p. 249

HUSEY

ROBERT of Duxbury; 1667 inventory, sworn by John Haward, does not mention any wife or family (MD 17:25); for further information see also MA PIONEERS p. 249

HYLAND/HILAND/HEYLAND

SAMUEL of Scituate; undated will, sworn 1677, names wife Isabel (PLYM COL PR 3:2:109); 1677/8 bond of administrator (PLYM COL RECS 5:254); for further information see also SCITUATE BY DEANE p. 290 (Note wife's name given wrongly.)

THOMAS Sr. of Scituate; 1682 will names son Thomas Hiland Jr. his executor, 1683 inventory (PLYM COL PR 4:2:33-5); for further information see also SCITUATE BY DEANE p. 290

THOMAS Jr. of Scituate; 1690/1 inventory sworn by "Thomas Hyland father of sd. deceased" (MD 30:71 or GEN ADV 1:117); for further information see also SCITUATE BY DEANE p. 290

Indians see:
  Great Harry, from Bristol County
  Hunter, Thomas of Titicut
  Numacke, Nanquit of "Pinquin Hole"
  Pamantaquash, the Pond Sachem
  Pompaquine, alias Jacob of Pokeesett
  Quonnukquosh of Satocett
  Sassamon, John

INGELL

BENJAMIN of Bristol; 1690 Bristol Co. will names wife Weightstill (GEN ADV 4:58); perhaps he is the Benjamin Ingalls in RI GEN DICT p. 208, column 1, and SAVAGE 2:519

IRISH

ELIAS of Taunton; 1677 bond of administrator William Witherell (PLYM COL RECS 5:247); for further information see also SAVAGE 2:524

JOHN of Duxbury; 1677/8 division of land "bequeathed" to sons Elias and John (PLYM COL RECS 5:252); for further information see also SAVAGE 2:524, DUXBURY BY WINSOR pp. 272-273, LITTLE COMPTON FAMS p. 370, BRIDGEWATER BY MITCHELL p. 401

Irishman, see MORE, CORNELIUS

JACKSON

HUGH of Barnstable; 1658/9 deposition re nuncupative will which bequeaths to Joshua Lambert (PLYM COL RECS 3:157); for further information see also PLYM COL RECS 3:151

SAMUEL of Scituate; 1682 will mentions unnamed wife and son Jonathan (PLYM COL PR 4:2:17); for further information see also MA PIONEERS p. 254, BARNSTABLE FAMS 2:113, SCITUATE BY DEANE p. 291

JAMES

JOHN of Scituate; married Lydia Turner, great-granddaughter of Pilgrim William Brewster; 1679 administration granted to widow Lydia James and her father John Turner (PLYM COL RECS 6:9, 43); settlement (MD 19:100); inventory (PLYM COL PR 4:1:63); for further information see also PLYM COL RECS 6:43, SCITUATE BY DEANE p. 293, MD 19:97-100

JENKINS

JOHN Sr. of Barnstable; 1683 will, probated 1685, names wife Mary (PLYM COL LR 5:386); for further information see also MA PIONEERS p. 258, BARNSTABLE FAMS 2:90

JOHN of Sandwich; 1684 inventory sworn by son Zacheriah Jenkins (PLYM COL PR 4:2:81 or PLYM SCRAP pp. 129-130); bond of administrator (PLYM SCRAP p. 44); for further information see also NARRA HIST REG 5:151, BARNSTABLE FAMS 2:90 (footnote), RI FAMS 1:564

SAMUEL, son of; 1673 inquest (PLYM COL RECS 5:130-131)

JENNEY

JOHN of Plymouth; came on the ship <u>Little James</u>; 1643 will names wife Sarah (MD 6:169-174); for further information see also MD 10:129, MQ 40:4:111, TAG 35:70, NEHGR 115:233, 119:234

SARAH of Plymouth; widow of John; came on the ship <u>Little James</u>; 1654 will names son Samuel Jenney (MD 8:171-175); for further information see also MA PIONEERS p. 258, PLYM COL RECS 4:43, 80, TAG 35:70

JONES

ROBERT of Swansea; probably son of Robert of Hingham; undated inventory made about 1676 lists estate in Swansea and was appraised by Edward Batter, Joell Jenkins, Zacherya Edy and Thomas Esterbroke (PLYM COL PR 3:2:68); 1677 settlement mentions unnamed wife (PLYM COL RECS 5:236); for further information see also MA PIONEERS p. 262, HINGHAM BY LINCOLN 2:387, TAG 31:96

SAMUEL probably of Rehoboth; 1662 bond of administrator John Kingsley of Rehoboth (PLYM SCRAP p. 18)

JOYCE

JOHN of Yarmouth; 1666 will, exhibited 1666/7, names wife Dorothy (MD 16:160; PLYM COL RECS 4:141); for further information see also TAG 43:1, MA PIONEERS p. 264

MISTRESS [Dorothy] of Yarmouth; widow of John; will approved 1679/80 (PLYM COL RECS 6:31); for further information see also TAG 43:1, AMERICAN COLONISTS BY SHERWOOD p. 48

KEMPE

WILLIAM of Duxbury; 1641 administration granted to Elizabeth Kempe (MD 4:75 or PLYM COL RECS 2:27, 37); for further information see also PLYM COL MARR p. 25, MA PIONEERS p. 265, DUXBURY BY WINSOR p. 273

KEMPTON/KEMTON

EPHRAIM Sr., of Scituate; 1645 inventory does not mention any names (MD 6:250); 1652 administration granted to Mannasses and Ephraim Kempton (PLYM COL RECS 3:17); for further information see also MA PIONEERS p. 265-6, PLYM COL RECS 2:85, 89, LITTLE COMPTON FAMS p. 385

EPHRAIM of Scituate; 1655 inventory (MD 14:112); 1656 administration granted to Joanna Kempton (PLYM COL RECS 3:17, 108); 1658 agreement re children of Ephraim and wife, both deceased (MD 12:213); for further information see also MA PIONEERS p. 265, SCITUATE BY DEANE pp. 299-300, LITTLE COMPTON FAMS p. 385

JOANNA of Scituate; widow of Ephraim; 1657 administration granted to Manasses Kempton (PLYM COL RECS 3:114, MD 14:113); for further information see also PLYM COL MARR p. 26, SCITUATE BY DEANE pp. 299-300

MANASSES Sr. of Plymouth; came on the ship _Anne_; 1665 report of estate supervisors that John Harding of Eastham had paid for land in Eastham which he bought of Manasses (PLYM COL LR 3:27); for further information see also MA PIONEERS p. 266, SAVAGE 3:8-9, MD 17:104

KING

DANIEL of Freetown; 1688 Bristol Co. will names brother Thomas King (GEN ADV 3:120)

THOMAS Sr. of Scituate; 1691 will names wife Anna (GEN ADV 2:105); for further information see also MA PIONEERS p. 270, SCITUATE BY DEANE p. 301

KINGMAN

JOHN Sr. of Bridgewater; 1690/1 Plymouth Co. inventory presented by widow Elizabeth Kingman (MD 30:184 or GEN ADV 2:59-60); for further information see also BRIDGEWATER BY MITCHELL p. 225, WEYMOUTH BY CHAMBERLAIN 3:356

KINGSLEY

ELDAD of Rehoboth; son of John; 1679 will names wife Mehitabel (PLYM COL PR 4:1:42, 43); for further information see also MA PIONEERS p. 271-272, SWANSEA HIST p. 171, SAVAGE 3:29

JOHN of Rehoboth; 1677 will, sworn 1678/9, names wife Mary and deceased wife Alice (PLYM COL PR 4:1:4, 5); land given to John French (PLYM COL RECS 6:4); for further information see also MA PIONEERS p. 272, SWANSEA HIST p. 171, SAVAGE 3:29, EARLY REHOBOTH 3:20-22, 4:32

KNAP(P)

AARON Sr. of Taunton; 1674 will names wife Elizabeth (MD 33:160); 1674 administration (PLYM COL RECS 5:153); for further information see also PLYM COL RECS 8:195, SAVAGE 3:33

JOSEPH of Plymouth; 1690/1 testimony re estate, 1691 inventory presented by brother Moses Knapp (MD 30:141, 142 or GEN ADV 1:119, 2:26); for further information see also PLYM ANC LANDMARKS 2:167

KNOT(T)

GEORGE of Sandwich; 1648 nuncupative will, exhibited 1649, names wife Martha (MD 9:157); for further information see also MA PIONEERS p. 274, CAPE COD HIST 2:46

MARTHA of Sandwich; widow of George; 1673 will names son Samuel Knott (MD 25:89); for further information see also MA PIONEERS p. 274

KNOWLES

JAMES; 1678 administration granted to brother Samuel of Eastham (PLYM COL PR 3:2:124); for further information see also PLYM COL RECS 7:268, NEHGR 79:292

KNOWLES con't

JOHN of Eastham; married Apphia Bangs; 1675 inventory and administration, with March 1676 [sic] inventory, sworn Oct. 1675 [sic] by widow Apthya Knowles (PLYM COL PR 3:2:6); 1676 mention of Widow Knowles (PLYM COL RECS 5:177, 200); new administrators in 1676/7, widow having married Steven Wood (PLYM COL RECS 5:220); for further information see also CAPE COD HIST 2:393, NEHGR 79:293, PLYM COL RECS 5:224

LAKE

Daughter of Richard of Yarmouth; 1672 inquest (PLYM COL RECS 5:94-5)

LANCKFORD

RICHARD of Plymouth; 1633 inventory sworn by Joshua Pratt, with Edward Winslow administrator (MD 1:83; PLYM COL RECS 1:18); for further information see also MA PIONEERS p. 278

LANDERS see LAUNDERS

LAPHAM

JOSEPH of Bridgewater; 1676 administration granted to Thomas Lapham of Scituate (PLYM COL RECS 5:213); for further information see also SCITUATE BY DEANE p. 302

THOMAS of Scituate; 1644 will, 1648 inventory sworn by widow Mary Lapham (MD 10:198; PLYM COL RECS 2:169); for further information see also MA PIONEERS p. 278, SCITUATE BY DEANE p. 302

LATHROP see LOTHROP

LAUNDER(S)/LANDERS

THOMAS of Scituate; 1675 inventory sworn by John Launder (PLYM COL PR 3:1:176); for further information see also MA PIONEERS p. 279, NEHGR 124:42-45

WILLIAM of Marshfield; 1648 will, exhibited 1648/9, names friends Thomas Burne and Robert Waterman executors (MD 9:82); for further information see also MA PIONEERS p. 279

LAYTHROPE see LOTHROP

LEE

MARY of Barnstable, widow; 1681 settlement on son[-in-law] John Howland (MD 11:32); for further information see also MA PIONEERS p. 282

LEICHFIELD

EXPERIENCE of Scituate; son of Lawrence; 1673 inquest (PLYM COL RECS 5:121-122); administration granted to Josiah Leichfield (PLYM COL RECS 5:132); distribution (PLYM COL RECS 5:139, 154); for further information see also SCITUATE BY DEANE p. 305, TAG 33:155

LENDALL see LINDALE

LEONARD/LEONARDSON/LONORSON

JAMES Sr. of Taunton; 1691 Bristol Co. settlement names widow Margaret Leonard (GEN ADV 4:123; NEHGR 63:327); for further information see also SAVAGE 3:79, TAG 10:200

SOLOMON of Bridgewater; married Sarah Chandler, granddaughter of Pilgrim James Chilton; 1675 settlement, with administration granted to Samuel Leanardson (PLYM COL RECS 5:179-180); for further information see also MF 2:10-11, TAG 27:5

SOLOMON of Bridgewater; son of above and great-grandson of Pilgrim James Chilton; 1686 inventory sworn by Mary Lenerson (GEN ADV 1:17 or PN&Q 4:1-2); for further information see also MF 2:24, BRIDGEWATER BY MITCHELL p. 244, DUXBURY BY WINSOR p. 275

LETTICE

THOMAS of Plymouth; 1678 will, acknowledged 1681, sworn 1682, names wife Anne (MD 14:64); for further information see also MA PIONEERS p. 284

LEWIS

GEORGE Sr. of Barnstable; undated will, sworn 1663, names wife Mary (MD 16:23); inventory (PLYM COL RECS 4:55); for further information see also MA PIONEERS p. 285, BARNSTABLE FAMS 2:115, HINGHAM BY LINCOLN 2:441, SCITUATE BY DEANE p. 303

GEORGE Jr. of Barnstable; son of George; 1683 settlement names widow Elizabeth Lewis (PLYM COL PR 4:2:124-125); for further information see also BARNSTABLE FAMS 2:129

LEWIS con't

JOHN Sr. of Barnstable; 1676 inventory (PLYM COL PR 3:1:174-175); 1676 settlement names his mother Mary Lewis (PLYM COL LR 4:43); for further information see also MA PIONEERS p. 285 and MA PIONEERS corrections p. 312a, BARNSTABLE FAMS p. 120

JOSEPH of Swansea; undated original inventory (PLYM SCRAP p. 111); undated inventory copy (PLYM COL PR 3:2:68); 1677 settlement, with administration granted to his widow Mary Jenkins (PLYM COL RECS 5:236); for further information see also SAVAGE 3:88, TAG 31:96, SCITUATE BY DEANE p. 303

NATHANIEL of Swansea; son of George; 1683 nuncupative will mentions daughter Mary and unnamed wife (PLYM COL PR 4:1:2); for further information see also SCITUATE BY DEANE p. 303

LINCOLN/LINCKON

THOMAS Sr. of Taunton; 1683 will names wife Elizabeth (PLYM COL PR 4:2:57); for further information see also MA PIONEERS p. 286, HINGHAM BY LINCOLN 3:20

LINCKS

PHILLIP of Scituate; 1638 administration granted to Timothy Hatherley (PLYM COL RECS 1:105); for further information see also MA PIONEERS p. 287

LINDALE

JAMES of Duxbury; 1652 will, sworn 1652/3, names wife Mary (MD 11:87); administration (PLYM COL RECS 3:22); for further information see also MA PIONEERS p. 287, DUXBURY BY WINSOR p. 276

MARY of Duxbury; widow of James; 1652/3 administration granted to Constant Southworth (PLYM COL RECS 3:22); inventory (MD 11:92); for further information see also DUXBURY BY WINSOR p. 276

LINNEL

DAVID of Barnstable; son of Robert; 1688 Barnstable Co. will, proved 1688/9, names wife Hannah (MD 10:100); for further information see also BARNSTABLE FAMS 2:148, MA PIONEERS p. 287, BARNSTABLE FAMS p. 148, SCITUATE BY DEANE p. 304

LINNEL con't

ROBERT of Barnstable; 1662 will mentions unnamed wife, but inventory was sworn by Pinninah Linell (MD 15:58); 1662/3 administration (PLYM COL RECS 4:31); for further information see also TAG 51:35, MA PIONEERS p. 287

LITCHFIELD see LEICHFIELD

LITTLE

THOMAS Sr. of Marshfield; married Anna, daughter of Pilgrim Richard Warren; 1671 will, exhibited 1672, with inventory sworn by widow Anna Little (MD 4:161; PLYM COL RECS 5:101); for further information see also MA PIONEERS p. 288, FAMS OF PILGRIMS (Warren family), LITTLE COMPTON FAMS p. 398

THOMAS Jr. of Marshfield and Taunton; son of Thomas; 1675 will, sworn 1676 names brother Samuel (MD 4:164); for further information see also MD 4:161, LITTLE COMPTON FAMS p. 398

LOE see LOW

LOMBARD see LUMBURT

LONORSON see LEONARDSON

LOTHROP/LAYTHROPE

JOHN, Reverend, of Barnstable; 1653 will mentions unnamed wife (MD 11:42); administration granted to "Mistress Laythorp" (PLYM COL RECS 3:46); for further information see also PLYM COL MARR p. 28, MA PIONEERS p. 292, BARNSTABLE FAMS 2:162-211, NEHGR 84:437

JOHN of Scituate; 1676/7 administration granted to Major Cudworth (PLYM COL RECS 5:221); for further information see also SCITUATE BY DEANE p. 168

MARK of Bridgewater; 1685 inventory sworn by son Samuel Lothrop (PLYM COL LR 5:385); administration (PLYM COL RECS 6:179-180); 1685/6 bond of administrator (PLYM SCRAP p. 55); for further information see also BRIDGEWATER BY MITCHELL p. 233, SAVAGE 3:121

LOTHROP/LAYTHROPE con't

MARK of Bridgewater; son of above Mark; 1690 Plymouth Co. will, sworn 1690/1, names brother Samuel Lothrop (MD 30:186 or GEN ADV 2:60)

LOW/LOE

ARTHUR of Marshfield; 1690/1 Plymouth Co. inventory sworn by sister Margaret Loe (MD 30:71 or GEN ADV 1:117); son chooses guardian (PLYM CO CT RECS 1:211); for further information see also SAVAGE 3:125, NGSQ (June 1983)

LUCAS

THOMAS of Plymouth; 1678 inventory (PLYM COL PR 4:1:14); 1678/9 inquest with settlement which mentions unnamed widow and son Benoni (PLYM COL RECS 6:5-7); for further information see also PLYM ANC LANDMARKS 2:179

LUMBERT

JOSHUA of Barnstable; 1689/90 Barnstable Co. will, probated 1691, names wife Abigail (MD 12:88); for further information see also TAG 52:137

THOMAS of Barnstable; 1662 will, 1664 inventory sworn by widow Joyce Lumbert (MD 16:124); administration (PLYM COL RECS 4:81); for further information see also TAG 52:136, BARNSTABLE FAMS 2:217

LUMPKIN

WILLIAM of Yarmouth; 1668 will, sworn 1671, names wife Tamasin (MD 12:139); inventory (PLYM SCRAP p. 93); for further information see also MA PIONEERS p. 295, YARMOUTH BY SWIFT p. 70

MacRAY see MUCKROY

MacKENNEY

DANIEL of Taunton; 1672 inquest (PLYM COL RECS 5:102); 1685 administration granted to John Hathway and Thomas Leonard (PLYM COL RECS 6:176); for further information see also PLYM COL RECS 3:168

MACOMBER/MAYCOMBER

MATHEW of Taunton; son of William; 1675 will, sworn 1676/7, gives all estate to brother John (PLYM COL PR 3:2:58); 1676 inventory (PLYM SCRAP p. 120); for further information see also MA PIONEERS p. 297

WILLIAM of Marshfield; 1670 inventory sworn by Ursilla, Thomas, and Mathew Maycomber (MD 18:187); for further information see also MA PIONEERS p. 297, TG 2:170ff (1981) [English ancestry and some descendants]

MAKEPEACE

WILLIAM of Taunton; son of Thomas; 1681 inquest and settlement (PLYM COL RECS 6:75, 79); inventory sworn by widow Anne Makepeace (PLYM COL PR 4:1:100); for further information see also MA PIONEERS p. 298

MAN(N)

NATHANIEL of Scituate; son of Richard; 1688 Plymouth Co. administration granted to his brother Thomas Mann (GEN ADV 1:41 or PN&Q 4:124); for further information see also TAG 52:169, SCITUATE BY DEANE p. 309

RICHARD of Scituate; 1655/6 inquest (PLYM COL RECS 3:92-93, 96, 98); administration granted to his unnamed widow (MD 14:23); 1675 receipts of sons (PLYM COL RECS 5:174); for further information see also MA PIONEERS p. 298, TAG 27:220, 52:166, MD 3:193-201, SCITUATE BY DEANE p. 309 [He did _not_ come on the _Mayflower_; it was Pilgrim Richard _More_ who did.]

MARSHALL

ROBERT of Plymouth; 1681 guardianship for son Robert (PLYM COL RECS 6:66); for further information see also PLYM ANC LANDMARKS 2:184

MARTIN

ABRAHAM of Rehoboth; 1669 will, exhibited 1670, names brother Richard (MD 19:32); for further information see also MA PIONEERS p. 302, HINGHAM BY LINCOLN 3:64

JOHANNA of Rehoboth; widow of Robert; 1669 adminstration granted to John Ormsbey (PLYM COL RECS 5:21); for further information see also MA PIONEERS p. 303

JOHN of Rehoboth; 1686/7 Bristol Co. adminstration granted to Henry Harrison and wife Katharine (GEN ADV 3:119); for further information see also REHOBOTH VR p. 848

ROBERT of Rehoboth; will, dated only the sixth of the 3rd month [May], names wife Joan, with inventory taken 19 June 1660 (MD 17:160); 1661/2 oath of Capt. Thomas Willett to "will and inventory" [the record book should probably have said that Willett was to take the oath of the widow on the inventory of her husband] (PLYM COL RECS 4:8; REHOBOTH VR p. 848); for further information see also MA PIONEERS p. 303, EARLY REHOBOTH 1:107

MASON

SAMPSON of Rehoboth; 1672 will, sworn 1676, names wife Mary (PLYM COL PR 3:2:49, 50); for further information see also SAVAGE 3:169, SWANSEA HIST p. 180

MATHEWES

JAMES of Yarmouth; 1684/5 administration granted to "Mr. Laythorpe and Mr. Thacher" (PLYM COL RECS 6:152); for further information see also MA PIONEERS p. 305, YARMOUTH BY SWIFT p. 66

THOMAS of Yarmouth; 1688 Barnstable Co. settlement names widow Sarah Mathewes (MD 10:6)

MAY

EDWARD of Plymouth; his second wife was Dorcas Billington, granddaughter of John of the ship *Mayflower*; 1691 inventory presented by widow Dorcas May, and settlement (MD 31:104; GEN ADV 2:106); for further information see also FAMS OF PILGRIMS (Billington family), TG 3:228ff

MAY con't

GEORGE of Boston and Swansea; 1681 inquest (PLYM COL RECS 6:75-76); settlement names widow Elizabeth May (PLYM COL PR 4:1:88-92); for further information see also SAVAGE 3:183

MAYCOMBER see MACOMBER

MAYO

JOHN of Yarmouth, minister; 1676 inventory, sworn by widow Tamasin Mayo, and settlement (MD 9:119-122; PLYM COL RECS 5:200); for further information see also MA PIONEERS p. 308, NEHGR 95:39, 103:32

NATHANIEL of Eastham; son of Rev. John; Nathaniel married Hannah Prence, granddaughter of Pilgrim William Brewster; 1661 will, proved 1661/2, names wife Hannah (MD 17:215); administration (PLYM COL RECS 4:8); for further information see also PLYM COL MARR p. 30, MA PIONEERS pp. 308-9, SAVAGE 3:188, FAMS OF PILGRIMS (Brewster family), CAPE COD HIST 2:362

WILLIAM of Eastham; son of John; married Elizabeth Ring, granddaughter of Pilgrim Stephen Hopkins; 1691 Barnstable Co. inventory mentions unnamed wife (MD 14:117); for further information see also FAMS OF PILGRIMS (Hopkins family)

MERRICK

WILLIAM Sr. of Eastham, Ensign; 1686 Barnstable Co. will names wife Rebecca (MD 10:7); for further information see also MA PIONEERS p. 311, DUXBURY BY WINSOR p. 282

MERRITT

HENRY of Scituate; 1653 inventory mentions his brother John Merritt (MD 11:198); administration (PLYM COL RECS 3:51); for further information see also MA PIONEERS p. 312, SCITUATE BY DEANE p. 311

JOHN of Scituate; 1676/7 inventory names widow Elizabeth Merritt (PLYM COL PR 3:2:68-69); inquest (PLYM COL RECS 5:227, 236); for further information see also MA PIONEERS p. 312 & 312a

MIGHELL

THOMAS of Scituate, minister; 1689 Plymouth Co. will, sworn 1689/90, names wife Bethulia (GEN ADV 1:74 or PN&Q 5:61); for further information see also SAVAGE 3:206, SCITUATE BY DEANE p. 194

MILES see MYLES

MILLARD/MILLER

JOHN Jr. of Rehoboth; 1684 inquest (PLYM COL RECS 6:142); inventory sworn by widow Elizabeth Millard (PLYM COL PR 4:2:75); for further information see also DSGR 23:58ff and REHOBOTH VR p. 852, SAVAGE 3:208

MILLER alias Hodgis

NICHOLAS of Plymouth; 1665 will bequeaths to Peter Reife and others, apparently not his kin (MD 16:157); for further information see also PLYM COL RECS 4:113, MA PIONEERS p. 234, TAG 35:178

MITCHELL

EXPERIENCE of Bridgewater; came on the ship _Anne_; married (1) Jane Cooke, daughter of Pilgrim Francis Cooke; 1684 Plymouth Co. will, sworn 1689, names wife Mary (GEN ADV 1:73-74; MD 4:150, but see MD 32:97 for correction of will year; MQ 27:3:3); for further information see also MA PIONEERS p. 313, NEHGR 127:94, TAG forthcoming, DUXBURY BY WINSOR p. 282, BRIDGEWATER BY MITCHELL p. 251

JACOB of Dartmouth; son of Experience who came on the ship _Anne_; 1675/6 appointment of Experience and Edward Mitchell as overseers, 1677/8 appointment of same two as guardians of children (PLYM COL RECS 5:188, 252); inventory sworn _1691_ by son Thomas (GEN ADV 2:60); for further information see also BRIDGEWATER BY MITCHELL p. 252, MD 21:185-186

MORE/MOORE

CORNELIUS, an Irishman; 1664 inventory (MD 16:127 or PLYM SCRAP pp. 34-35); 1664/5 administration granted to Barnard Lumbert of Barnstable (PLYM COL RECS 4:81)

GEORGE of Scituate; 1677/8 inquest (PLYM COL RECS 5:250); for further information see also SCITUATE BY DEANE p. 313

MORTON

JOHN Sr. of Middleboro; son of George; came on the ship Anne; 1673 nuncupative will, with inventory sworn by widow Lettice Morton (MD 24:135, 25:123; PLYM SCRAP pp. 112-113); for further information see also PLYM COL MARR p. 52, SAVAGE 3:244, MD 11:93, MIDDLEBORO BY WESTON p. 48

NATHANIEL of Plymouth; came on the ship Anne; 1685 will names wife Ann (PLYM COL LR 5:350); for further information see also SAVAGE 3:244, CHARLESTOWN BY WYMAN 2:688, BRIDGEWATER BY MITCHELL p. 403

MUCKROY

JOHN; 1681 administration granted to Barnabas Laythorp (PLYM COL RECS 6:66)

MULLINS

WILLIAM of Plymouth; came on the ship Mayflower; 1620/1 nuncupative will names wife Alice (MD 1:230, NEHGR 42:62, or MQ 34:1:9); for further information see also WATERS 1:254, MQ 39:83, AMERICAN COLONISTS BY COLDHAM p. 41, FAMS OF PILGRIMS (Alden family, revised 1983)

MYLES

JOHN of Swansea, minister; 1682/3 will names wife Anne who swore to the inventory, dated only 18 May [no year] (PLYM COL PR 4:2:23, 24); for further information see also SAVAGE 3:259, EARLY REHOBOTH 3:115 footnote, HARVARD GRADS 3:287

NASH

SAMUEL of Duxbury; 1681 will names daughter Martha Clarke (PLYM COL PR 4:2:112); 1683/4 inventory (PLYM COL RECS 6:125-126); for further information see also MA PIONEERS p. 324, BRIDGEWATER BY MITCHELL p. 404, TAG 15:165-167, DUXBURY BY WINSOR p. 284

Negroes see Blacks

NELSON

MARTHA of Plymouth, widow; came on the ship Fortune; 1683/4 administration granted to John Nelson (PLYM COL RECS 6:124); inventory (PLYM COL PR 4:2:74); for further information see also TAG 42:39, 56:32

WILLIAM Sr. of Plymouth; 1679 will, sworn 1679/80, names wife Martha (PLYM COL PR 4:1:54-56); 1683/4 inventory (PLYM SCRAP p. 42); for further information see also MA PIONEERS p. 326, TAG 42:39, 56:32

NEWLAND

JEREMIAH of Taunton; 1695 settlement to widow Katherine Newland, "Jeremy Newland of Taunton [having] about 15 years since died intestate" (NEHGR 63:227); 1701 settlement of estate of Jeremiah and Katherine on their children (BRISTOL CO PR 2:67-68); for further information see also MA PIONEERS p. 327, Taunton VR

NEWMAN

JOANNA of Dorchester, lately of Rehoboth; widow of Rev. Noah Newman; 1678 will, sworn 1679, appoints her unnamed mother executrix (SUFFOLK CO PROBATE OLD SERIES 9:341); inventory on her daughter's estate was sworn in 1680 by Mrs. Margery Flint (SUFFOLK CO PROBATE OLD SERIES 9:22); for further information see also SAVAGE 3:275

NOAH of Rehoboth, Pastor; son of Rev. Samuel; 1678 will names wife Joanna (PLYM COL PR 3:2:118-119); for further information see also MA PIONEERS p. 328, SAVAGE 3:275

NEWMAN con't

SAMUEL Sr. of Rehoboth; 1661 will, sworn 1663, names wife Sibil (MD 15:234); 1663/4 administration granted to widow and son Samuel Newman (PLYM COL RECS 4:54); for further information see also MA PIONEERS p. 328

NICARSON

NICHOLAS of Yarmouth; son of William; 1681/2 inventory sworn by widow Mary Nicarson (PLYM SCRAP p. 21); administration and settlement (PLYM COL PR 4:2:27, 32 or PLYM COL RECS 6:99); for further information see also MA PIONEERS p. 329, CAPE COD HIST 2:207

Child; 1667 inquest on unnamed child of NICHOLAS and MARY of Yarmouth (PLYM COL RECS 4:170)

NICOLLS

JAMES of Capt. John Allen's company "put on shore upon Cape Codd"; 1667 inquest at Eastham (PLYM COL RECS 4:176)

NUMACKE

NANQUIT, an Indian of "Pinquin Hole," [in Plymouth]; 1669 will, sworn by Richard Bourne of Sandwich, mentions unnamed wife (MD 19:30)

ORMSBEY

JACOB of Rehoboth; son of Richard; 1671 [sic] administration granted to widow and her brother John Perrin, with settlement, 1677 inventory sworn by widow Mary Ormsbey (PLYM COL PR 3:2:81, 83, 84); for further information see also MA PIONEERS p. 336, SAVAGE 3:316, EARLY REHOBOTH 1:112

RICHARD of Rehoboth; 1664 inventory sworn by widow Sarah Ormsby (MD 16:127); 1665 administration and settlement (PLYM COL RECS 4:105, 164, 167); for further information see also MA PIONEERS p. 336

OTIS

HANNAH of Scituate; daughter of John below; 1685 will, probated 1688, names mother Mary (GEN ADV 1:19 or PN&Q 4:108)

JOHN of Scituate; 1683/4 will and codicil, sworn 1684, names wife Mary (PLYM COL PR 4:2:78-80); for further information see also SCITUATE BY DEANE p. 318, SCITUATE BY PRATT p. 369, SAVAGE 3:323, HINGHAM BY LINCOLN 3:102

PABODIE see PAYBODY

PACKARD see also PARKER

SAMUEL of Bridgewater; 1684 will, sworn 1684/5, names wife Elizabeth (MD 15:254); for further information see also BRIDGEWATER BY MITCHELL p. 264, HINGHAM BY LINCOLN 3:104, SAVAGE 3:327, WEYMOUTH BY CHAMBERLAIN 4:454

PADDOCK

ROBERT of Plymouth; 1650 agreement of widow Mary Paddock to adoption of her son (PLYM COL RECS 12:198); for further information see also MA PIONEERS p. 338, PLYM COL MARR p. 33, DUXBURY BY WINSOR p. 286

PAINE

ALICE; her 1672 will calls her wife of Stephen Paine Sr. of Rehoboth, and mentions deceased husband William Parker, but the 1682 inventory says she is "of Taunton" (PLYM COL PR 4:2:38, 39); for further information see also PLYM COL RECS 8:85

JOHN of Boston; 1679 bond of administrators Richard Thayer and Increase Robinson re Taunton Iron Works (PLYM SCRAP p. 13); 1679/80 debt, 1681 execution against his property (PLYM COL RECS 6:79-80, 7:222-223); for further information see also SAVAGE 3:333

STEVEN Sr. of Rehoboth; 1679 will names wife Elizabeth (PLYM COL PR 4:1:37-41); for further information see also REHOBOTH VR p. 857, SAVAGE 3:335

STEVEN Jr. of Rehoboth; undated document names wife Anna and eldest son Steven Paine, letter from Steven Sr. (father of the deceased) and 1678 inventory (PLYM COL PR 3:2:110-114); for further information see also REHOBOTH VR p. 857, SAVAGE 3:335

PAKES see PEAKS

PALMER

JOHN Sr. of Scituate; 1675 will, exhibited 1676, names eldest son John Jr. and others (PLYM COL PR 3:1:158); for further information see also MA PIONEERS p. 341-342, HINGHAM BY LINCOLN 3:105

PALMER con't

SAMUEL of Scituate; son of John; 1676 settlement (PLYM COL PR 3:2:26, 27); 1676 administration granted to John Palmer (PLYM COL RECS 5:211); for further information see also SCITUATE BY DEANE pp. 319-320

THOMAS Sr. of Scituate; 1689 inventory sworn by son Thomas (GEN ADV 1:73 or PN&Q 5:21); [SCITUATE BY DEANE has several errors]

WILLIAM the younger, of Plymouth; came on the ship Fortune; 1636 inventory (PLYM SCRAP p. 9); 1637/8 complaint of John Willis and wife Elizabeth, formerly wife of William Palmer the younger (PLYM COL RECS 7:7); for further information see also TAG 32:41, LITTLE COMPTON FAMS p. 445

WILLIAM the elder of Duxbury and Plymouth; came on the ship Fortune; will, dated 1637, mentions young unnamed wife and designates William Bradford and others executors (MD 2:147); will sworn 1637/8 (PLYM COL RECS 1:78); 1653/4 distribution to Moses Rowley (PLYM COL RECS 3:45-6); for further information see also TAG 32:39, LITTLE COMPTON FAMS p. 444

WILLIAM of Dartmouth; 1675 inventory (PLYM COL PR 4:1:32); 1679 administration granted to widow Susan Palmer, settlement (PLYM COL RECS 6:13); for further information see also TAG 32:44, LITTLE COMPTON FAMS p. 445

PAMANTAQUASH

alias THE POND SACHEM; undated will, with 1668 note, names son William and others (PLYM COL RECS 12:229)

PARKER see also PACKARD

JOHN of Taunton; 1665 will names wife Sarah, inventory taken 1667/8 (MD 17:26); for further information see also MA PIONEERS p. 344

NATHANIEL of Scituate; son of William; 1690/1 Plymouth Co. petition of his mother Mary Parker and brother Miles (MD 30:72-73 or GEN ADV 1:117-8); for further information see also SCITUATE BY DEANE p. 320, TAG 41:105

PARKER con't

ROBERT of Barnstable; 1684/5 administration, 1685/6 settlement (PLYM COL RECS 6:153, 183); inventory sworn by widow Patience (PLYM COL LR 5:390); for further information see also NEHGR 112:190

WILLIAM of Taunton; 1659 will names wife Alice, 1661 inventory (MD 17:216); administration (PLYM COL RECS 4:16); receipt of heir (MD 18:64); for further information see also MA PIONEERS p. 345

WILLIAM of Scituate; 1684 will names wife Mary (PLYM COL PR 4:2:76-77); for further information see also TAG 41:102, SCITUATE BY DEANE p. 320

PARTRIDGE

RALPH of Duxbury; 1655 will, probated 1658, names daughter Elizabeth Thacher executrix (MD 14:228); bond of William Collier (PLYM COL RECS 3:134); for further information see also MA PIONEERS p. 347, DUXBURY BY WINSOR p. 171

PAYBODY

JOHN of Duxbury; grandson of Pilgrim John Alden; 1649 will, sworn 1667, names wife Isabel (MD 17:23); 1669 inquest (PLYM COL RECS 5:29); for further information see also FAMS OF PILGRIMS (Alden family), DUXBURY BY WINSOR p. 285, LITTLE COMPTON FAMS p. 436

PEABODY see PAYBODY

PEAKS/PAKES

JUDITH of Scituate; 1685 will names deceased husband William Peaks (PLYM COL PR 4:2:150-1); will sworn (PLYM COL RECS 6:176); for further information see also MA PIONEERS p. 350, TAG 33:155

THANKFUL; child of William; 1655 inquest (PLYM COL RECS 3:92)

WILLIAM of Scituate; 1682 will, 1683 inventory sworn by his widow Judith Peaks (PLYM COL PR 4:2:40-1); for further information see also MA PIONEERS pp. 312b, 350, SCITUATE BY DEANE p. 321

PEARCE/PEIRCE/PIERCE etc.

ABRAHAM Sr. of Duxbury; 1673 administration granted to Abraham Jr., and settlement with his siblings (PLYM COL RECS 5:116-117); for further information see also TAG 54:164 (English ancestry etc.), DUXBURY BY WINSOR p. 288, MA PIONEERS p. 360, MQ 49:57-67

JAMES of Boston; 1660 inquest (PLYM COL RECS 3:195-196)

MICHAEL, of Scituate, Capt.; slain in King Philip's War; 1675[/6] will, inventory and addition (PLYM COL PR 3:2:8, 10); 1675/6 original will, sworn 1676, names wife Anna (PLYM SCRAP p. 128-9); son's guardian appointed (PLYM COL RECS 5:213); settlement (PLYM COL RECS 5:208); for further information see also SCITUATE BY PRATT p. 325, SCITUATE BY DEANE p. 325, HINGHAM BY LINCOLN 3:108

PECK(E)

JOSEPH Sr. of Rehoboth; undated will, exhibited 1663, names sons Nicholas and Samuel executors (MD 15:236); 1663/4 administration (PLYM COL RECS 4:55); for further information see also MA PIONEERS p. 351, RI FAMS 1:626, NEHGR 89:327

NATHANIEL of Swansea; probably son of Joseph; 1676 inventory and children's guardianships (PLYM COL PR 3:2:29, 109); 1676 administration granted to Jonathan Bosworth Sr. and Samuel Peck and settlement (PLYM COL RECS 5:212, 259); administrators sell land (PLYM COL RECS 6:56, 73); for further information see also MA PIONEERS p. 351

PEIRCE see PEARCE

PERREN

JOHN Sr. of Rehoboth; 1674 will names wife Anna (MD 34:35); for further information see also MA PIONEERS p. 355, EARLY REHOBOTH 1:109, NEHGR 96:256

PERREY/PERRY

ANTHONY of Rehoboth; 1682 will names wife Elizabeth, 1682/3 inventory (PLYM COL PR 4:2:29-30); witnesses sworn (PLYM COL RECS 6:103 [Edward is probably an error for Anthony]); for further information see also SAVAGE 3:399

PERREY/PERRY con't

EZRA Sr. of Sandwich; 1689 Barnstable Co. will, probated 1690, inventory sworn by his widow Elizabeth Perry (MD 11:26); for further information see also NEHGR 115:86

SARAH of Sandwich; 1659 executorship granted to Ezra Perrey (PLYM COL RECS 3:163); inventory (PLYM SCRAP p. 15)

PETCOCK/PIDCOCK

GEORGE of Scituate; 1670 will turns his estate over to the town (MD 19:31); for further information see also MA PIONEERS p. 359, DUXBURY BY WINSOR p. 292, SCITUATE BY DEANE p. 324

PETERSON

JOHN of Duxbury; grandson of Pilgrim George Soule; 1690 Plymouth Co. inventory sworn by his brother John Peterson (GEN ADV 1:114 or PN&Q 5:115); for further information see also MF 3:10

PHELPS see also PHILLIPS

Daughter of Thomas of Yarmouth; 1673 inquest (PLYM COL RECS 5:122)

THOMAS of Yarmouth; 1673 inventory mentions unnamed children, and 1674 appraisal mentions "the woman," probably meaning his wife (MD 33:161); 1674 settlement of estate of "Thomas Phelps alias Phillips" mentions unnamed widow and grants administration to Hugh Stewart (PLYM COL RECS 5:153)

PHIBENS

PHILLIP of Scituate; 1684 inventory taken by town selectmen (PLYM SCRAP p. 47); for further information see also CIVEN

PHILLIPS see also PHELPS

FAITH of Marshfield; wife of John Phillips and widow of Pilgrim Edward Doty; 1675 will names husband John Phillips (MD 3:89); settlement (PLYM COL RECS 5:239); for further information see also MA PIONEERS p. 358

PHILLIPS con't

JAMES of Taunton; probably son of William; 1677 settlement names widow Mary (PLYM COL PR 3:2:79, 83); for further information see also SAVAGE 3:411, NEHGR 110:225

JOHN Jr.; probably of Marshfield, son of John who married Faith; 1658 inquest (PLYM COL RECS 3:148); for further information see also GEN ADV 3:28, DUXBURY BY WINSOR p. 291

THOMAS of Yarmouth, see PHELPS, THOMAS

WILLIAM of Taunton; 1654 will names wife Elizabeth (MD 12:244); for further information see also MA PIONEERS p. 358, NEHGR 110:225

PHINNEY see FINNEY

PICKLES

JONAS of Scituate; 1665 administration granted to Thomas Roes of Scituate and "his wife" (PLYM COL RECS 4:106); nuncupative will, sworn 1665, mentions unnamed wife, inventory sworn 1665 by Allis Roes (MD 16:156); for further information see also MD 2:33, SCITUATE BY DEANE p. 323

PIDCOCK see PETCOCK

PIDDELL

WILLIAM of Capt. John Allen's company "put on shore upon Cape Codd"; 1667/8 inquest at Eastham (PLYM COL RECS 4:176)

PIERCE see PEARCE

PILBEAME

JAMES of Rehoboth; 1653 inventory, administration granted to son-in-law Lenard Ryce [sic, should be Rice Leonard] (MD 14:23); for further information see also MA PIONEERS p. 361, EARLY REHOBOTH 3:130

PITNEY

JAMES Sr., probably of Marshfield; 1663 will, exhibited 1664, names daughter Sarah Thomas executrix (MD 16:25); inventory (PLYM SCRAP p. 24); for further information see also MA PIONEERS p. 363, SAVAGE 3:442

POINTING

THOMAS of Taunton; 1680 inventory mentions unnamed brother (PLYM COL PR 4:1:99); administration granted to Phillip Pointing (PLYM COL RECS 6:43)

POLLARD

GEORGE of Duxbury; apparently not related to George of Marblehead; 1671 power of attorney of John Pollard of England, "eldest brother and heir" of George deceased (PLYM COL LR 3:205); for further information see also PLYM COL RECS 2:41, DUXBURY BY WINSOR p. 292

POMPAQUINE

alias Jacob of Pokeesett; 1679 permission granted to William Numacke to sell his lands (PLYM COL RECS 6:19)

PONTUS

WILLIAM of Plymouth; 1650 will, sworn 1652, names son-in-law James Glass (MD 11:92); for further information see also MA PIONEERS p. 366

POOLE

ELIZABETH of Taunton; 1654 will, exhibited 1656, names brother Capt. William "Pole" (MD 14:24); for further information see also TAG 31:120, MA PIONEERS p. 367, TAG 14:222, 31:120, ASPINWALL RECS p. 41

TIMOTHY; son of William; 1667 inquest (PLYM COL RECS 4:170); for further information see also MA PIONEERS p. 367

POPE
THOMAS of Dartmouth; 1683 will, with 1683/4 administration granted to Isaac and Seth Pope (MD 18:129, PLYM COL RECS 6:122); for further information see also MA PIONEERS p. 368, PLYM COL RECS 5:244

PRATT
BENAJAH of Plymouth; son of Joshua below; 1682 inventory sworn by widow Persis Pratt (PLYM SCRAP p. 25-6 or PLYM COL PR 4:2:12-13); for further information see also PLYM ANC LANDMARKS 2:209, TAG 30:145, PLYM CH RECS 1:249

JOSHUA of Plymouth; came on the ship Anne; 1656 administration granted to Bathsheba Pratt, and inventory (PLYM COL RECS 3:108, MD 14:113); for further information see also MA PIONEERS p. 371

PRENCE/PRINCE
THOMAS, Gov. of Plymouth Colony; came on the ship Fortune; 1672 will, with 1673 codicil, names wife Mary, receipts of heirs (MD 3:203, 33:98 or MQ 33:3:73); for further information see also MA PIONEERS p. 372, CAPE COD HIST 2:363, DUXBURY BY WINSOR p. 293

PRIOR see PRYOR

PRITCHARD
RICHARD "sometimes of Charlestown"; 1668/9 Middlesex Co. will names wife Margery (CHARLESTOWN BY WYMAN 2:777); 1678 receipts of heirs (PLYM COL PR 4:1:16-17)

PRYOR
JOSEPH of Duxbury; son of Thomas; 1690/1 inventory sworn by brother John Pryor (MD 30:141, GEN ADV 2:26); for further information see also DUXBURY BY WINSOR p. 294

THOMAS of Scituate; 1639 will names son John executor (MD 3:76); inventory sworn (PLYM COL RECS 1:141); son's guardian (PLYM COL RECS 2:77); for further information see also MA PIONEERS p. 375, SCITUATE BY DEANE p. 328

QUONNUKQUOSH

Indian man of Satocett [probably the present town of Harwich]; 1681 will, acknowledged by the testator in 1682 names sons Conkkequid and Ercemas (MD 22:187)

RAMSDEN/RAMSDELL

JOSEPH of Lakenham (then in Plymouth, now in Carver); his first wife was Rachel, daughter of Pilgrim Francis Eaton; 1674 inventory (MD 8:18-20, PLYM SCRAP p. 119); for further information see also MF 1:6-7

RAWLINS

NATHANIEL of Scituate; son of Thomas; 1662 inventory sworn by widow Lydia Rawlins (MD 15:62); guardianship (PLYM COL RECS 6:23); administration (PLYM COL RECS 4:46); for further information see also SCITUATE BY DEANE p. 330

READ

JOHN Jr.; 1676 inventory at Rehoboth sworn by his widow Rachel, undated settlement (PLYM COL PR 3:2:39, 110); 1676 administration granted to widow Rachel and others (PLYM COL RECS 5:200); for further information see also SAVAGE 3:516 [MA PIONEERS p. 380 confuses father and son], WEYMOUTH BY CHAMBERLAIN 4:564

JOHN of Rehoboth; 1679 will, sworn 1685, names wife Sarah (PLYM COL LR 5:360); for further information see also SAVAGE 3:516, WEYMOUTH BY CHAMBERLAIN 4:564

REDWAY

JAMES Jr. of Rehoboth; son of James below; 1676 administration granted to John Reddaway (PLYM COL RECS 5:221); 1676/7 settlement and Rehoboth inventory (PLYM COL PR 3:2:77); for further information see also MA PIONEERS p. 381, EARLY REHOBOTH 1:135, NEHGR 98:175

JAMES of Rehoboth; 1677 will, sworn 1684, names son John executor (PLYM COL PR 4:2:72-3); for further information see also MA PIONEERS p. 381, EARLY REHOBOTH 1:125, NEHGR 98:163

REIFE see RIFFE

REW

EDWARD of Taunton; 1678 will names wife Sarah (PLYM COL PR 3:2:124-5); for further information see also TAG 54:97

RICHMOND

JOHN Sr. of Taunton; 1663 will, probated 1669, names son John executor (MD 18:248); receipts of heirs (MD 19:60); for further information see also MA PIONEERS 392a, TAG 36:137, 54:96, LITTLE COMPTON FAMS p. 511, RI FAMS 1:750

JOHN Jr. probably of Taunton; 1672 inquest (PLYM COL RECS 5:101); for further information see also TAG 54:97

RICKARD

GILES Sr. of Plymouth; 1684 will, sworn 1684/5, names wife Hannah (PLYM COL PR 4:2:101-2); for further information see also MA PIONEERS p. 385, NEHGR 111:172, TAG 30:145, 31:215

HANNAH of Plymouth, widow of John Churchill Sr. and of Giles Rickard Sr.; 1691 inventory sworn by Joseph Churchill, receipts of heirs (MD 30:142, GEN ADV 2:59); for further information see also PLYM ANC LANDMARKS 2:213, TAG 30:145, 31:215

JOHN Sr. of Plymouth; son of Giles; 1678 administration granted to widow (H)ester Rickard and son John Rickard (PLYM COL PR 3:2:122-3); for further information see also MA PIONEERS p. 385, NEHGR 112:154

THOMAS of Scituate; 1648 will names Thomas Pincin executor (MD 9:155); for further information see also MA PIONEERS p. 385

RIDER/RYDER

SAMUEL Sr. of Yarmouth; 1679 will, sworn 1679/80, names wife Anne (PLYM COL PR 4:1:45-6); for further information see also MA PIONEERS p. 385, YARMOUTH BY SWIFT p. 60, MD 11:49, 170, TAG 43:117

ZACHARIAH of Yarmouth; 1685 will, sworn 1685/6, names wife Mary (PLYM COL LR 5:380); for further information see also MD 27:37, YARMOUTH BY SWIFT p. 61

RIFFE/REIFE

PETER, probably of Plymouth; 1683/4 administration granted to William Hoskens (PLYM COL RECS 6:124); for further information see also Nicholas Miller entry

RING

MARY of Plymouth, widow; undated will, probated 1631, names son Andrew etc. (MD 1:29); for further information see also TAG 42:193

ROBINS/ROBBINS

JOHN; bond of widow Jehosabath Robins to administer estate of John of Plymouth (PLYM SCRAP p. 91); 1669/70 administration (PLYM COL RECS 5:33); 1669 inventory of estate of John of Bridgewater (PLYM SCRAP p. 86); for further information see also BRIDGEWATER BY MITCHELL p. 299

NICHOLAS of Duxbury; 1650 will names wife Ann (MD 10:22); for further information see also MA PIONEERS p. 386, DUXBURY BY WINSOR p. 297

ROBINSON

ISAAC Jr. of Barnstable; 1668 inquest (PLYM COL RECS 5:7); for further information see also BARNSTABLE FAMS 2:230, MARTHA'S VINEYARD BY BANKS 2:60-62, 3:418-419, TAG 18:45, 56:147

THOMAS of Scituate; 1676/7 inquest (PLYM COL RECS 5:226); for further information see also NEHGR 111:16, SCITUATE BY DEANE p. 332

WILLIAM of Rehoboth; 1690 Bristol Co. will, proved 1691, names brothers George and Benjamin executors (GEN ADV 4:59)

ROCKETT

JOSEPH of Rehoboth; 1683 nuncupative will names wife Mary (PLYM COL PR 4:2:140); for further information see also SAVAGE 3:556-7

ROGERS

HANNAH of Bristol [then Massachusetts, now Rhode Island]; widow of John Brown of Salem, and wife of John Rogers, grandson of Pilgrim Thomas Rogers; 1691 will appoints her brothers Gershom and Nehemiah Hobart overseers (MD 20:2); for further information see also MF 2:164, FAMS OF PILGRIMS

JAMES of Eastham; grandson of Pilgrim Thomas Rogers; 1678 bond of his widow Mary Rogers as administratrix (PLYM COL RECS 5:265); undated settlement, administration, inventory (PLYM COL PR 3:2:121); for further information see also MF 2:163

JOHN Sr. of Marshfield; not of the Mayflower family; 1660 will, exhibited 1661, names wife Frances (MD 17:214); receipts of heirs (MD 3:254, PLYM COL LR 4:39); for further information see also MARSHFIELD BY RICHARDS 2:11, MA PIONEERS p. 389

JOSEPH Sr. of Eastham, Lt.; came on the ship Mayflower with father Thomas Rogers; 1677 will, sworn 1677/8, names wife Hannah (MD 3:67); 1678 administration (PLYM COL RECS 5:271); for further information see also PLYM COL RECS 2:155, MF 2:155 MQ 28:1:16, 37:84

JOSEPH Jr., perhaps of Eastham; 1660/1 oath of his widow Susannah Rogers to inventory (PLYM COL RECS 3:206); 1663/4 administration (PLYM COL RECS 4:55); for further information see also MF 2:157

THOMAS of Eastham; grandson of Pilgrim Thomas Rogers; 1678 inventory (PLYM COL PR 3:2:131); 1704 settlement names deceased eldest son Joseph (MD 11:179); for further information see also MF 2:160

ROLLOCKE

ROBERT of Sandwich; 1669 inventory and administration granted to widow Sissillie [Cecily?] Fish of Sandwich (MD 18:248, PLYM COL RECS 5:28); inventory (PLYM SCRAP p. 82)

ROSE/ROWS/ROUSE

ANNIS of Marshfield; widow of John; 1687 will, probated 1688, names son John executor (GEN ADV 1:41-2 or PN&Q 4:124-125); for further information see also MA PIONEERS p. 392

JOHN of Marshfield; 1676/7 inquest (PLYM COL RECS 5:226)

JOHN Sr. of Marshfield; 1682 will, with 1684 inventory sworn by widow Annis Rouse in 1685 (PLYM COL PR 4:2:106-7); for further information see also MA PIONEERS p. 392, LITTLE COMPTON FAMS p. 528

ROWLEY

HENRY of "Suckienessett" (Falmouth); his son married Elizabeth Fuller, daughter of Matthew Fuller (PLYM COL MARR p. 39); 1673 inventory sworn by Moses Rowley (MD 24:137); original inventory (PLYM SCRAP p. 101); for further information see also FAMS OF PILGRIMS (Edward Fuller family) [very confused account in MA PIONEERS p. 393]

ROWS see ROSE

RUSSELL

GEORGE of Scituate; 1668 deposition re nuncupative will made about 13 years earlier (PLYM COL LR 3:113, 128); 1673 agreement of John Hudson and wife Ann, formerly wife of George Russell (PLYM COL LR 3:243); for further information see also SCITUATE BY DEANE p. 334, HINGHAM BY LINCOLN 3:142

SAMUEL of Scituate; 1675/6 will, sworn 1676, names wife Mary (PLYM COL PR 3:1:168); 1676 administration (PLYM COL RECS 5:201); for further information see also SCITUATE BY DEANE p. 335, MARTHA'S VINEYARD BY BANKS 2:70-71

RYDER see RIDER

SABERRY see SEABURY

SABIN

HEZEKIAH of Rehoboth; see Noah below (REHOBOTH VR p. 874)

NEHEMIAH of Rehoboth; 1676 inventory sworn by widow Sarah Sabin (PLYM COL PR 3:2:32); administration (PLYM COL RECS 5:200); for further information see also SAVAGE 4:1, NEHGR 99:241

NOAH, probably of Rehoboth; son of William; 1691 Bristol Co. inventory sworn by administrator James Sabin (NEHGR 62:351); division of the estates of Noah and Hezekiah among their siblings NEHGR 63:228)

WILLIAM of Rehoboth; 1685 Suffolk Co. will, sworn 1687, chooses unnamed wife and son James executors (SUFFOLK CO PROBATE OLD SERIES #1582); for further information see also MA PIONEERS p. 396, EARLY REHOBOTH 3:128

SALE/SAILS

REBECCA of Rehoboth; "late wife of Edward"; 1664/5 inquest reports she hanged herself (PLYM COL RECS 4:83); for further information see also MA PIONEERS p. 397, REHOBOTH VR p. 874, TAG 21:243-245, MARTHA'S VINEYARD BY BANKS 2:130-132

SALSBERY

SUSANNA; widow of William; 1684 bond of William Salsbery of Swansea as administrator (PLYM COL RECS 6:145-146); inventory (PLYM COL PR 4:2:146); for further information see also MA PIONEERS p. 392a

SAMSON/SAMPSON

HENRY of Duxbury; came on the ship Mayflower; 1684 will, sworn 1684/5, appoints son Stephen executor (MD 2:142 or MQ 27:2:12, or MAY RDR p. 114); for further information see also FAMS OF PILGRIMS, TAG 28:5, 52:207, 56:141, DUXBURY BY WINSOR p. 300

SAMSON/SAMPSON con't

SAMUEL of Duxbury; son of Abraham; not a Mayflower line; 1678 inventory sworn by widow Esther, and undated settlement mentions her expected marriage to John Soule (PLYM COL PR 3:2:108, 120, 124); 1683/4 Samuel's son chooses guardian (PLYM COL RECS 6:125); for further information see also DUXBURY BY WINSOR p. 301, TAG 28:3, MF3:7 [but Esther was not a Nash, but probably a Delano]

SANDERS/SANDERSON

HENRY of Sandwich; 1685 settlement mentions unnamed widow and unnamed children (PLYM COL RECS 6:169); undated inv. taken by Thomas Tupper and Samuel Briggs (PLYM SCRAP p. 110); for further information see also NEHGR 127:250

SANDERSON see SANDERS

SARES see SEARS

SARGENT/SERJANT

WILLIAM of Barnstable; 1679/80 will names wife Sarah, 1682/3 inventory (PLYM COL PR 4:2:19-20); for further information see also MA PIONEERS p. 400

SAVAGE

JOHN of Rehoboth; 1678 settlement names widow Sarah Savage (PLYM COL RECS 5:271); inventory (PLYM COL PR 4:1:6); for further information see also SAVAGE 4:24

SAVORY

THOMAS Sr. of Plymouth; 1674 will, exhibited 1676, names wife Anne (PLYM COL PR 3:1:172); 1675/6 administration (PLYM COL RECS 5:189); for further information see also MA PIONEERS p. 402

SCUDDER

JOHN of Barnstable; 1690 Barnstable Co. settlement names widow Hannah Scudder (MD 11:27); for further information see also BARNSTABLE FAMS 2:233

SEABURY/SABERRY

JOHN of Duxbury; he married Martha Pabodie, granddaughter of Pilgrim John Alden; 1678 bond of administrator brother Samuel Seabury (PLYM SCRAP p. 130-131); for further information see also LITTLE COMPTON FAMS p. 538, FAMS OF PILGRIMS (Alden family)

SAMUEL of Duxbury; son of John; 1680 will mentions deceased former wife, and present wife Martha, 1681 inventory (PLYM COL PR 4:1:93, 96); 1682 guardianships of children (PLYM COL RECS 6:91, 97); for further information see also MA PIONEERS p. 405, DUXBURY BY WINSOR p. 305, FAMS OF PILGRIMS (Alden family), LITTLE COMPTON FAMS p. 538, HARVARD GRADS 1:574

SEALIS

RICHARD of Scituate; 1653 will, exhibited 1656, names wife Egline (MD 13:94); for further information see also MA PIONEERS p. 405, SCITUATE BY DEANE p. 336

SEARS/SAERS

RICHARD of Yarmouth; 1667 will, sworn 1676, names wife Dorothy (PLYM COL PR 3:2:53-55); 1676 oath to will and inventory (PLYM COL RECS 5:213); for further information see also MA PIONEERS p. 406, YARMOUTH BY SWIFT p. 62, TAG 58:246

ROBERT of Rehoboth; 1677 inventory taken by Samuel Newman and Thomas Ormsbe (PLYM SCRAP p. 126)

SERJANT see SARGENT

SHAW

THOMAS of Barnstable; 1672 will names kinsman Robert Parker (MD 19:162); for further information see also MA PIONEERS p. 410

SHELLEY

JOHN of Barnstable; son of Robert; 1669 assumption of estate by father (PLYM COL RECS 5:27); for further information see also MD 18:60

SHEPHERD

WILLIAM of Taunton; 1663/4 will names eldest son Samuel Shepherd, with 1665 bond of administrator (PLYM SCRAP p. 45); inventory (MD 16:127); for further information see also MA PIONEERS p. 412

SHERMAN

WILLIAM of Marshfield; son of William; he married Desire, daughter of Pilgrim Edward Doty; 1680 inventory (PLYM SCRAP p. 18 or PLYM COL PR 4:1:80); 1681/2 bond names his children (PLYM SCRAP pp. 20-21 or MD 4:171); 1681/2 settlement names widow Desire who has married Israel Holmes (PLYM COL RECS 6:80 or MD 4:173); for further information see also MARSHFIELD BY RICHARDS 2:71 [MA PIONEERS pp. 413 & 250a confuses father and son; all data is on son]

SHOVE

GEORGE of Taunton, Rev.; 1687 Suffolk Co. will names wife Sarah (SUFFOLK CO PROBATE OLD SERIES 10:141-143); for further information see also MA PIONEERS p. 414, HARVARD GRADS 1:554

SHURTLEFF

WILLIAM of Marshfield; 1666 bond of administratrix, widow Elizabeth Shurtleff (PLYM SCRAP pp. 54-55); for further information see also MA PIONEERS p. 414 (under Shirtley), LITTLE COMPTON FAMS p. 569

SILVESTER/SYLVESTER

JOSEPH of Scituate, Capt.; 1690 Plymouth Co. deposition re nuncupative will names wife Mary (MD 30:138 or GEN ADV 1:118); 1691/2 settlement (PLYM CO CT RECS 1:216); for further information see also MA PIONEERS p. 444, SCITUATE BY DEANE p. 349, NEHGR 85:261-263

NAOMI of Scituate; widow of Richard; 1668 inventory (MD 17:110); 1669 bond of John Silvester to administer (PLYM SCRAP pp. 79-80); for further information see also MA PIONEERS p. 444, NEHGR 85:247, WEYMOUTH BY CHAMBERLAIN 4:631

SILVESTER/SYLVESTER con't

RICHARD Sr. of Marshfield; 1663 will names wife Naomi (MD 15:60); 1663 bond of administratrix (PLYM SCRAP p. 24); court provides for widow (PLYM COL RECS 4:46); guardians of children (PLYM COL RECS 5:50, 52); for further information see also MA PIONEERS p. 444, SCITUATE BY DEANE p. 347, DUXBURY BY WINSOR p. 324, NEHGR 85:247, WEYMOUTH BY CHAMBERLAIN 4:631

SIMMONS/SYMONS

MOSES of Duxbury; came on the ship Fortune; 1689 Plymouth Co. will names son John executor (MD 31:60 or GEN ADV 2:89-90); for further information see also MA PIONEERS p. 415 (first paragraph only), LITTLE COMPTON FAMS p. 571

MOSES Jr. of Scituate; son of Moses of the ship Fortune; 1676 will, exhibited 1676/7, mentions "wife", with inventory sworn by Patience Symons (PLYM COL PR 3:2:62-63); administration (PLYM COL RECS 5:220); 1683/4 son chooses guardian (PLYM COL RECS 6:125); for further information see also SAVAGE 4:100 [very confused account in MA PIONEERS p. 415]

MOSES of Scituate; son of Moses and grandson of Moses of the ship Fortune; 1690 Plymouth Co. will, sworn 1690/1, appoints brother John executor (GEN ADV 1:116 or MD 30:69); for further information see also SCITUATE BY DEANE p. 339, a confused account

SISSON

RICHARD of Dartmouth; 1683 will, sworn 1683/4, names wife Mary (PLYM COL PR 4:2:129, 131); for further information see also RI GEN DICT p. 181

SLOCUM

JOHN of Taunton; son of Anthony; 1651 inquest (PLYM COL RECS 2:174); for further information see also SAVAGE 4:107 (information on Anthony)

SMALLEY

Child; 1667/8 inquest on unnamed child kept by JOHN Sr. of Eastham (PLYM COL RECS 4:177); for further information see also CAPE COD HIST 2:359

SMITH

FRANCIS of Taunton; 1679 will names wife Sarah (PLYM COL PR 4:1:47-48); order to Mr. Brown and Mr. Smith to prove will (PLYM COL RECS 6:24); for further information see also MA PIONEERS p. 419

HENRY of Rehoboth; 1647 will mentions unnamed wife and son Daniel (MD 10:159); for further information see also MA PIONEERS p. 420, HINGHAM BY LINCOLN 3:152

HENRY of Rehoboth, Ensign; 1677 inventory sworn by his widow Elizabeth (PLYM COL PR 4:1:10); undated appointment, between 1677 documents, of Lt. Hunt and Nathaniel Paine (PLYM COL PR 3:2:83); 1678/9 settlement with administration (PLYM COL RECS 6:3-4); for further information see also SAVAGE 4:116

JAMES of Seacunke [Seekonk]; 1653 Suffolk Co. bond of administrator Amos Richardson (SUFFOLK CO PROBATE OLD SERIES #131)

JEREMIAH probably of Plymouth; son of John and Bennett; 1649/50 adoption by Thomas and Winifred Whitney (PLYM COL RECS 12:181); for further information see also MA PIONEERS p. 422, NEHGR 123:229

JOHN Sr. of Taunton; 1691 Bristol Co. will names son John (GEN ADV 4:124); for further information see also NEHGR 63:327

JOHN Jr. of Eastham; 1678 inventory sworn by his widow Hannah Smith (PLYM COL PR 4:1:12); 1678/9 settlement (PLYM COL RECS 6:5); for further information see also SAVAGE 4:122, TAG 40:194

JUDITH of Rehoboth; widow of Henry; 1650 will, exhibited 1651, (MD 10:172); for further information see also MA PIONEERS p. 420

RALPH of Eastham; 1685 administration granted to his widow Grace Smith and son Samuel Smith (PLYM COL RECS 6:175); 1685 bond of administrators (PLYM SCRAP p. 54); inventory names two sons (PLYM COL LR 5:362); for further information see also MA PIONEERS p. 423

SMITH con't

RICHARD and wife RUTH of Sandwich; 1684 inventory sworn by Benjamin Smith (PLYM SCRAP p. 46 or PLYM COL PR 4:2:81); 1684 administration on Richard's estate (PLYM COL RECS 6:145); for further information see also MA PIONEERS p. 423

SAMUEL of Taunton; 1679/80 settlement mentions unnamed "widow," with Mr. Brown and Mr. Smith to help settle estate (PLYM COL RECS 6:32); for further information see also SAVAGE 4:132

SNOW

JABEZ of Eastham, Lt.; grandson of Pilgrim Stephen Hopkins; 1691 Barnstable Co. inventory sworn by his widow Elizabeth Snow (MD 12:39, 22:165); for further information see also FAMS OF PILGRIMS (Hopkins family)

JAMES of Bridgewater; grandson of Pilgrim Peter Brown; 1691 inventory (GEN ADV 2:62); administration granted to his brother Benjamin Snow (MD 31:17); for further information see also FAMS OF PILGRIMS (Brown family)

NICHOLAS of Eastham; came on the ship Anne; married Constance, daughter of Pilgrim Stephen Hopkins; 1676 will, sworn 1676/7, names wife Constant (MD 3:167); 1676/7 administration (PLYM COL RECS 5:220); for further information see also FAMS OF PILGRIMS (Hopkins family), TAG 14:229, CAPE COD HIST 2:365, NEHGR 47:81

SOANE

WILLIAM of Scituate; 1671 will, sworn 1672, names wife Dorothy; agreement between William Tubbs and widow who plan to marry (MD 19:132, 143); for further information see also SCITUATE BY DEANE p. 338, NEHGR 70:260, 133:97

SOULE

GEORGE Sr. of Duxbury; came on the ship Mayflower; 1677 will, with codicil, appoints son John executor (MD 2:81 or MQ 28:3:11 or MAY RDR p. 74); for further information see also MF 3:3, MQ 45:189, DUXBURY BY WINSOR p. 310, BRIDGEWATER BY MITCHELL p. 408, NEHGR 124:121

SOULE con't

ZACHARIAH of Duxbury; son of Pilgrim George Soule; 1663 inventory (MD 5:110 or MAY RDR p. 392); 1663 bond of widow Margaret Soule (PLYM SCRAP p. 20); for further information see also MF 3:6

ZACHARIAH of Duxbury; grandson of Pilgrim George Soule; 1690/1 inventory sworn by his father John (MD 8:186 or GEN ADV 2:26); for further information see also MF 3:7

SOUTHWORTH

CONSTANT Esq. of Duxbury; 1678 will names wife Elizabeth, 1678/9 inventory (PLYM COL PR 4:1:18-20); for further information see also MA PIONEERS p. 426, LITTLE COMPTON FAMS p. 627, NEHGR 97:359, BRIDGEWATER BY MITCHELL p. 319, DUXBURY BY WINSOR p. 314

THOMAS, of Plymouth, Capt.; 1669 will mentions unnamed wife in "poor condition", with inventory sworn by son-in-law Joseph Howland (MD 18:185); for further information see also MA PIONEERS p. 426

SPARROW

RICHARD of Eastham; 1660 will, exhibited 1660/1, names wife Pandora (MD 12:57); for further information see also MA PIONEERS 426, CAPE COD HIST 2:361

SPOONER

WILLIAM of Dartmouth; 1683 will appoints son Samuel executor (PLYM COL PR 4:2:71); for further information see also TAG 45:121, 46:64

SPRAGUE

JOHN of Duxbury; 1676 inventory (PLYM COL PR 3:2:5); 1677 bond of his widow Ruth Sprague as administratrix (PLYM COL RECS 5:237-238); for further information see also TAG 41:178, DUXBURY BY WINSOR p. 317

STACY

RICHARD of Taunton; 1687 Bristol Co. administration granted to Thomas Lincoln Jr. (GEN ADV 3:119); for further information see also MA PIONEERS p. 429

STANDISH

DAVID of Duxbury; grandson of Pilgrim Myles Standish; 1689 inquest (PLYM CO CT RECS 1:191); for further information see also FAMS OF PILGRIMS, NEHGR 87:155

MILES Sr. of Duxbury; came on the ship Mayflower; 1655 will, exhibited 1656, names wife Barbara (MD 3:153 or MQ 26:4:12 or MAY RDR p. 200); 1657 administration granted to Alexander and Josiah Standish and "their mother" Barbara Standish (PLYM COL RECS 3:114); for further information see also FAMS OF PILGRIMS, MQ 36:2:58-59, NEHGR 68:339, 87:149, BRIDGEWATER BY MITCHELL p. 322, DUXBURY BY WINSOR p. 320

STANLAKE/STANLECK

DANIEL of Scituate; 1638 nuncupative will mentions unnamed wife and "my two children" (MD 3:77); will sworn in 1639/40 (PLYM COL RECS 1:141); for further information see also MA PIONEERS p. 430, SCITUATE BY DEANE p. 344

DANIEL of Scituate; 1684 inquest (PLYM COL RECS 6:141)

RICHARD of Scituate; 1691 will, with codicil, names wife Lydia (GEN ADV 2:90-91 or MD 31:62); for further information see also SCITUATE BY DEANE p. 345

STEPHENS/STEVENS

EDWARD of Marshfield; 1689 Plymouth Co. will names eldest son William (GEN ADV 1:113-114 or PN&Q 5:114); for further information see also SAVAGE 4:185

FRANCIS Sr. of Rehoboth; 1669 administration granted to Francis Jr. (PLYM COL RECS 5:21); 1669 inventory (PLYM SCRAP p. 76 or MD 17:117); for further information see also SAVAGE 4:185

RICHARD Jr. of Taunton; 1685 verdict regarding his death by "misadventure" (PLYM COL RECS 6:171, 175); for further information see also SAVAGE 4:188

STETSON

JOHN of Scituate, Ensign; son of Robert; 1690/1 Plymouth Co. inventory presented by his widow Abigail Stetson (GEN ADV 1:118-119 or MD 30:139); settlement (MD 30:140); for further information see also MA PIONEERS p. 434, SAVAGE 4:183

MATTHEW of Scituate; son of Benjamin; 1690 Plymouth Co. inventory sworn by his father Benjamin Stetson in 1690/1 (MD 30:72-73 or GEN ADV 1:117-118); for further information see also SCITUATE BY DEANE p. 341

STEVENS see STEPHENS

STOCKBRIDGE

CHARLES of Scituate; 1683 inventory (PLYM COL PR 4:2:70); 1685 settlement names widow Abigail Stockbridge (PLYM COL RECS 6:156-158); 1689/90 guardianships for children (PLYM CO CT RECS 1:203); 1694 suits of sons and administrators (PLYM SCRAP pp. 78, 80); for further information see also NEHGR 133:100, 187, SCITUATE BY PRATT p. 331, SCITUATE BY DEANE p. 342, TAG 38:186

STOUGHTON

SARAH of Taunton; 1691 Bristol Co. will names husband Nicholas (GEN ADV 4:123); for further information see also TAG 54:97-98

STREET

FRANCIS of Taunton; 1665 inventory (PLYM SCRAP pp. 43-44); inventory sworn by widow Elizabeth Street (MD 16:156); for further information see also SAVAGE 4:222

STURGIS

EDWARD Jr. of Yarmouth; married Temperance Gorham, granddaughter of Pilgrim John Howland; 1678 nuncupative will, sworn 1678 (PLYM COL PR 4:1:26-27); 1679/80 settlement names widow Temperance, now wife of Thomas Baxter (PLYM COL RECS 6:32 or PLYM COL LR 4:372); 1694 division (MD 23:61); for further information see also FAMS OF PILGRIMS (Howland family)

STURGIS con't

SAMUEL of Yarmouth; son of Edward but not the Edward above; 1674 inventory (PLYM COL PR 3:1:167); 1674/5 administration granted to his widow Mary Sturgis (PLYM COL RECS 5:160); inventory (PLYM COL PR 3:1:167); for further information see also MA PIONEERS p. 440

STURTIVANT

SAMUEL of Plymouth; 1669 inventory (PLYM SCRAP p. 83); 1669 will appoints unnamed wife executor and names sons and son-in-law executors (MD 18:188); for further information see also MA PIONEERS p. 440

SUTTON

JOHN of Rehoboth; 1672 inventory (MD 19:165); 1673 administration granted to his widow Julia Sutton and Nathaniel Paine (PLYM COL RECS 5:116); for further information see also NEHGR 91:61

JULIAN; widow of John of Rehoboth; 1678 inventory (PLYM COL PR 3:2:107); 1678 nuncupative will names son-in-law John Fitch (PLYM COL PR 3:2:110); for further information see also PLYM COL RECS 5:116, NEHGR 91:61

SWIFT

JOAN of Sandwich; widow of William; 1663 bond of William Swift as administrator (PLYM SCRAP p. 29); 1662 will, with 1664 deposition, appoints son William executor (MD 16:210); 1663/4 will sworn (PLYM COL RECS 4:55); for further information see also MA PIONEERS p. 443

WILLIAM of Sandwich; 1642 inventory (MD 4:168); 1642/3 administration granted to his widow Joan Swift (PLYM COL RECS 2:53, 54); for further information see also MA PIONEERS p. 443

SYLVESTER see SILVESTER

SYMONS see SIMMONS

TALBOT

MOSES of Plymouth; 1634 deposition regarding his death (MD 2:10-11)

TAYLOR

RICHARD of Yarmouth; 1673 bond of administrators (PLYM SCRAP p. 114); account names son John Taylor (MD 25:39); settlement (PLYM COL RECS 5:137); son's guardianship (PLYM COL RECS 5:146); for further information see also MA PIONEERS pp. 447-448, CAPE COD HIST 2:207, YARMOUTH BY SWIFT p. 67

RICHARD'S WIFE [Ruth]; 1673 inquest (PLYM COL RECS 5:123)

TERRY

THOMAS of Freetown; he married (H)annah Rogers, granddaughter of Pilgrim Thomas Rogers; 1691 will names wife "Hana" (BRISTOL CO PR 6:275-277); for further information see also MF 2:165-166

THACHER/THATCHER

ANTHONY of Yarmouth; 1667 inventory (MD 17:25); 1667 agreement between widow Elizabeth and her children (PLYM COL LR 3:112); administration (PLYM COL RECS 4:168, 175); for further information see also MA PIONEERS p. 449, TAG 58:245

JUDAH, of Yarmouth; son of Anthony; 1676 settlement (PLYM COL RECS 5:217); inventory (PLYM SCRAP p. 123 or PLYM COL PR 3:2:60); 1676/7 administration granted to widow Mary Thacher and others (PLYM COL RECS 5:220); for further information see also SAVAGE 4:272, CAPE COD HIST 2:194

THATCHER see THACHER

THOMAS

DAVID Sr. of Middleboro; 1689 inventory sworn by his widow Joanna (GEN ADV 1:73 or PN&Q 5:21); for further information see also MIDDLEBORO BY WESTON p. 53

THOMAS con't

NATHANIEL of Marshfield, Capt.; son of William; 1674 inventory sworn by Mistress Mary Thomas (MD 34:35); administration and agreement (PLYM COL RECS 5:158); for further information see also MA PIONEERS p. 451

WILLIAM of Marshfield; 1651 will names son Nathaniel executor (MD 10:162); for further information see also MA PIONEERS p. 451, DUXBURY BY WINSOR p. 325

THORP

JOHN; 1633 inventory presented by his widow Alice says he is of Plymouth (MD 1:158); order for inventory calls him of Duxbury (PLYM COL RECS 1:18, 20); for further information see also MA PIONEERS p. 452

THRESHER

CHRISTOPHER of Taunton; 1678 will, exhibited 1679, names wife Katheren (PLYM COL PR 4:1:29); for further information see also MA PIONEERS p. 453

TIFFANY

HUMPHREY of Rehoboth; 1685 administration granted to his widow Elizabeth Tiffany (PLYM COL RECS 6:175); for further information see also SAVAGE 4:300, NEHGR 105:166

TILDEN

JOSEPH of Scituate; 1670 will names wife Elizabeth (MD 18:186); account (PLYM COL RECS 5:118-121); administration (PLYM COL RECS 5:37); for further information see also PLYM COL RECS 5:102, 172, 180, SCITUATE BY DEANE p. 353, SCITUATE BY PRATT p. 380

NATHANIEL of Scituate; 1641 will names wife Lydia (MD 3:220); for further information see also MA PIONEERS p. 454, SCITUATE BY DEANE p. 353, AMERICAN COLONISTS BY COLDHAM p. 58, NEHGR 65:33, 75:226

TILSON

EDWARD, probably of Plymouth; his inventory sworn by Joan Tilson in 1660 (MD 17:160); administration (PLYM COL RECS 3:207); for further information see also MA PIONEERS p. 455 [Edmund and Edward seem to be the same man]

TILSON con't

JOHN of Scituate; son of Edward; 1673 nuncupative will names his brother Ephraim (MD 24:134-137 or PN&Q 4:6); administration (PLYM COL RECS 5:134); bond of administrator (PLYM SCRAP p. 116); for further information see also PLYM ANC LANDMARKS 2:263, PN&Q 4:6

TINKHAM

EPHRAIM Sr. of Plymouth; married Mary Brown, daughter of Pilgrim Peter Brown; 1683/4 will, proved 1685, names wife Mary (MD 4:122 or MAY RDR p. 282); for further information see also FAMS OF PILGRIMS (Brown family), MA PIONEERS p. 456, TAG 33:214, 42:40, NGSQ 67:253

TISDALE/TISDALL

JOHN Sr. of Taunton; undated will, probated 1676, names "wife" executrix and mentions eldest son John (MD 21:29-34); administration and settlement (PLYM COL RECS 5:212, 219); for further information see also MA PIONEERS p. 456, PLYM COL RECS 5:224, DUXBURY BY WINSOR p. 326

JOHN Jr. of Taunton; married Hannah Rogers, granddaughter of Pilgrim Thomas Rogers; 1677/8 bond of administratrix widow Anne Tisdal (MD 21:34-35 or PLYM COL RECS 5:251-253); guardianship (PLYM COL PR 3:2:93); for further information see also MF 2:165-166

TITUS

JOHN Sr. of Rehoboth; 1688/9 Bristol Co. will, proved 1689, names wife Abigail (GEN ADV 3:121); for further information see also REHOBOTH VR p. 881, SAVAGE 4:308

TOOTO

Negro man; 1691 Barnstable Co. will, sworn 1691/2, names James Gorham and Mr. Baxter executors (MD 12:188)

TORREY

JAMES of Scituate, Lt.; bond of widow Anne Torrey as administratrix, and original inventory (PLYM SCRAP pp. 40, 46); 1665 inventory (MD 16:157); administration (PLYM COL RECS 4:106, 110); for further information see also MA PIONEERS p. 458, SCITUATE BY PRATT p. 322, SCITUATE BY DEANE p. 358

TOTMAN

MARY; wife of Thomas of Scituate; 1666 inquest (PLYM COL RECS 4:130); for further information see also SCITUATE BY DEANE p. 356, TAG 41:103

THOMAS of Scituate; 1678 inquest (PLYM COL RECS 5:262); for further information see also SCITUATE BY DEANE p. 356, TAG 41:103

TRACY

STEPHEN of Great Yarmouth, England, formerly of Duxbury; came on the ship Anne; 1654/5 power of attorney, recorded 1656, names son John and other children (MD 10:143); for further information see also TAG 51:71, 242, MA PIONEERS p. 460, DUXBURY BY WINSOR p. 326

TREBEY

PETER; son of Peter of Newport RI; 1672 inquest mentions his mother Bethya Trebey (PLYM COL RECS 5:101); for further information see also SAVAGE 4:328

TREUANT

JOSEPH of Marshfield; 1684 inquest (PLYM COL RECS 6:147); 1685 inventory sworn by his widow Hannah Treuant (PLYM COL PR 4:2:109); for further information see also SAVAGE 4:334

MORRIS of Marshfield; 1678 will, sworn 1685, names wife Jane (PLYM COL PR 4:2:104-105); for further information see also MA PIONEERS p. 462, MARSHFIELD VR p. 17

TUBBS

WILLIAM Sr. of Duxbury; 1677 will, probated 1688, names wife Dorothy (PN&Q 4:108 or GEN ADV 1:19); for further information see also MA PIONEERS p. 463, DUXBURY BY WINSOR p. 327

TURNER

HUMPHREY of Scituate; 1669 will, sworn 1673, names sons Young John Turner and Nathaniel Turner executors (MD 24:42); for further information see also MA PIONEERS p. 464, SCITUATE BY PRATT p. 314, SCITUATE BY DEANE p. 360, TAG 19:231

TURNER con't

ISRAEL of Scituate; son of John & Ann (James) Turner; 1689 inventory sworn by his widow Sarah Turner (PN&Q 5:20 or GEN ADV 1:73); for further information see also SCITUATE BY DEANE p. 361, SAVAGE 4:345, NEHGR 133:193

JAPHETH of Duxbury; son of John & Ann (James) Turner; 1690 inventory, presented by his widow Hannah Turner (PN&Q 5:117-118 or GEN ADV 1:115); settlement (PLYM CO CT RECS 1:210); for further information see also SCITUATE BY DEANE p. 361, SAVAGE 4:346

JOHN of Barnstable; 1667 inventory mentions Mistress Dimacke's account (MD 17:24); 1671 settlement to Mathew Darby (MD 19:61); administration granted to Thomas Huckens (PLYM COL RECS 4:151, 153); [information in MA PIONEERS p. 464 is wrong]

JOHN of Scituate; 1686 Suffolk Co. will, exhibited 1687, calls himself son of Humphrey, and names sons Japhet and Israel executors (SUFFOLK CO PROBATE OLD SERIES 10:177, 281); for further information see also SCITUATE BY DEANE p. 361 (under "Young son John")

LAZARUS of Scituate; son of Daniel; 1690/1 Plymouth Co. inventory sworn by brother Eliab Turner (MD 30:72 or GEN ADV 1:117); for further information see also SCITUATE BY DEANE p. 361

THOMAS Sr. of Scituate; 1688 will names eldest son Nathan Turner and others (PN&Q 5:19 or GEN ADV 1:42); for further information see also MA PIONEERS p. 465, SCITUATE BY DEANE p. 361

UTLEY

[SAMUEL] of Scituate; in 1662 his unnamed widow was to swear to his inventory (PLYM COL RECS 4:16, 22); for further information see also SCITUATE BY DEANE p. 363

VENOR
TIMOTHY; 1681 inquest (PLYM COL RECS 6:75-76)

VIALL
JOHN of Swansea; 1681 Suffolk Co. will and codicil, sworn 1686, names wife Elizabeth (SUFFOLK CO PROBATE OLD SERIES 11:34, #1566); will judged void (PLYM COL RECS 6:199-200); inventory (SUFFOLK CO PROBATE OLD SERIES #1566 or TAG 22:264); for further information see also NARRA HIST REG 3:97, RI FAMS 2:224

VINALL
ANNA of Scituate; widow of Stephen; 1664/5 administration granted to Stephen and John Vinall (PLYM COL RECS 4:81); inventory (MD 16:127); for further information see also MA PIONEERS p. 471, SCITUATE BY DEANE p. 364, SCITUATE BY PRATT p. 374

VIXEN see WIXAM

WADE

NICHOLAS of Scituate; 1683 will mentions unnamed wife (PLYM COL PR 4:2:136-137); inventory sworn by his widow Elizabeth Wade (PLYM SCRAP p. 32); for further information see also MA PIONEERS p. 472, SCITUATE BY DEANE p. 370

WADSWORTH

CHRISTOPHER of Duxbury; 1677 will, exhibited 1680, names wife Grace (PLYM COL PR 4:1:68-71); for further information see also MA PIONEERS p. 472 [but not slain in 1676], SAVAGE 4:379, DUXBURY BY WINSOR p. 328

GRACE of Duxbury; widow of Christopher; 1687 Plymouth Co. will, proved 1688, names son John Wadsworth executor (GEN ADV 1:20 or PN&Q 4:123); for further information see also MA PIONEERS p. 472

JOSEPH of Duxbury; son of Christopher; 1689 will, sworn 1690, names wife Mary (PN&Q 5:118 or GEN ADV 1:115); for further information see also DUXBURY BY WINSOR p. 328

WALDRON

ISAAC of Boston, physician; 1685/6 administration granted to John Usher of Boston (PLYM COL RECS 6:179); for further information see also SAVAGE 4:389, PLYM COL RECS 5:149, PLYM COL LR 5:235

WALKER

ELIZABETH; two-year old daughter of Philip of Rehoboth; 1664/1665 inquest (PLYM COL RECS 4:83)

JOHN; young servant of Robert Latham of Marshfield; 1654/5 inquest (PLYM COL RECS 3:71)

JOHN of Marshfield; 1663 inventory sworn by his widow Lydia Walker in 1664 (MD 16:128); for further information see also PLYM COL MARR p. 48, SAVAGE 4:394, NGSQ (June 1983)

MICHAEL of Rehoboth; 10 year-old son of Philip; 1677 inquest (PLYM COL RECS 5:209)

WALKER con't

PHILLIP, deacon of Rehoboth; administration granted to widow Jane Walker (PLYM COL RECS 6:28); 1679 settlement order (PLYM COL RECS 6:27); settlement (BRISTOL CO PR 2:43-46); inventory (PLYM COL PR 4:1:34-35); for further information see also SAVAGE 4:395, EARLY REHOBOTH 3:25-52, TAG 41:207

WALLIS

HENRY of Duxbury; 1641 settlement of his land on John Irish (PLYM COL RECS 2:12); for further information see also DUXBURY BY WINSOR p. 332, MA PIONEERS p. 476

WALLEY

THOMAS Jr. of Sandwich; son of Thomas; 1672 will names wife Hannah (MD 19:164); for further information see also SAVAGE 4:401

THOMAS, Rev. of Barnstable; pastor of Barnstable church; 1677 will names wife Sarah Walley (PLYM COL PR 3:2:115); for further information see also SAVAGE 4:400-401, CAPE COD HIST 2:274

WARREN

ELIZABETH of Plymouth; widow of Pilgrim Richard Warren; came on the ship Anne; 1673/4 settlement to son Joseph and others (PLYM COL RECS 5:139, 140; MD 25:13); for further information see also MA PIONEERS p. 480, FAMS OF PILGRIMS, MQ 42:125-128, 43:12-16

JOSEPH Sr. of Plymouth; son of Pilgrim Richard Warren; 1689 will names wife Priscilla (MD 4:14 or MAY RDR p. 237 or GEN ADV 1:43); for further information see also FAMS OF PILGRIMS

NATHANIEL of Plymouth; son of Pilgrim Richard Warren; 1667 will names wife Sarah (MD 2:36 or MAY RDR p. 61); administration (PLYM COL RECS 4:168); for further information see also FAMS OF PILGRIMS, TAG 51:92

RICHARD of Plymouth; came on the ship Mayflower; 1653 settlement (MD 2:64); widow receives his rights (PLYM COL RECS 1:54); for further information see also FAMS OF PILGRIMS, MQ 42:125-128, 43:12-16

WASHBOURNE

BENJAMIN of Bridgewater; son of John and great-grandson of Pilgrim Francis Cooke; 1690 nuncupative will, sworn 1690/1, administered by his brothers Joseph and Samuel (GEN ADV 2:60 or MD 16:47); for further information see also BRIDGEWATER BY MITCHELL p. 340, PN&Q 5:2

JOHN Sr. of Bridgewater; son of John; married Elizabeth Mitchell, granddaughter of Pilgrim Francis Cooke; 1686 will, sworn 1687, names wife Elizabeth (GEN ADV 2:25 or MD 15:248); for further information see also BRIDGEWATER BY MITCHELL p. 339-339, MD 16:248, SAVAGE 4:429, FAMS OF PILGRIMS (Cooke family), TAG forthcoming

WATERMAN

ROBERT of Marshfield; 1652 inventory (MD 11:100); 1652/3 administration granted to widow Elizabeth Waterman (PLYM COL RECS 3:22, 174-175); guardians of children appointed (PLYM COL RECS 4:113); for further information see also MA PIONEERS p. 481, DUXBURY BY WINSOR p. 333

WATSON

ELKANAH of Plymouth; son of George; 1689/90 inventory sworn by his widow Mercy Watson (GEN ADV 1:113 or PN&Q 5:109 [corrects errors in GEN ADV]); for further information see also PLYM COL RECS 8:16, SAVAGE 4:437, PLYM ANC LANDMARKS 2:277

GEORGE of Plymouth; 1688 inventory sworn by his son Elkanah (GEN ADV 1:43 or PN&Q 5:20); for further information see also PLYM COL MARR p. 49, MA PIONEERS p. 482, PLYM ANC LANDMARKS 2:277

THOMAS of Duxbury; 1639 will bequeaths estate to niece Anna Watson, daughter of John Watson deceased (LECHFORD'S NOTEBOOK p. 199 [original p. 125]); for further information see also MA PIONEERS p. 482, LECHFORD'S NOTEBOOK p. 194 [original p. 122]

WAYMOUTH

TITUS; 1656 inquest, inventory and account mentions unnamed "heirs" and possessions in Boston and Virginia (PLYM COL RECS 3:109-110)

WELLS

ISACKE of Barnstable; 1673 will, sworn 1673/4, names wife Margaret executrix (MD 25:89); for further information see also MA PIONEERS p. 486, SCITUATE BY DEANE p. 379

MARGARET of Barnstable, widow; 1675 administration granted to John Miller and Isaac Chapman (PLYM COL RECS 5:180); inventory (PLYM COL PR 3:1:166); for further information see also MA PIONEERS p. 486

WEST

NATHANIEL of Rhode Island; 1658/9 inquest (PLYM COL RECS 3:158); for further information see also RI GEN DICT p. 218

SAMUEL of Duxbury; 1689 inventory sworn by his widow Tryphosa West (PN&Q 5:110 or GEN ADV 1:113); for further information see also BRIDGEWATER BY MITCHELL p. 409, DUXBURY BY WINSOR p. 334

WESTON

EDMOND of Duxbury; 1686 will names son Elnathan executor (MD 15:187); for further information see also MA PIONEERS p. 487, NEHGR 41:285, MD 15:186, NGSQ 71:41-63

WETHERELL/WITHERELL

JOHN of Scituate, Lt.; 1690 will, sworn 1690/1, names wife Hannah executrix (MD 31:16, GEN ADV 2:61-62); for further information see also SCITUATE BY DEANE p. 193, TAG 32:194-195

SAMUEL of Scituate; son of William; 1684 settlement, bond of administratrix widow Isabel Wetherell (PLYM COL RECS 6:133); 1683/4 inventory (PLYM COL PR 4:2:133); guardians of children (PLYM CO CT RECS 1:203); for further information see also MA PIONEERS p. 488, SCITUATE BY DEANE p. 193

WILLIAM of Scituate, pastor; 1684 will names daughter-in-law Isabell Wetherell, widow of son Samuel, executrix (PLYM COL PR 4:2:132-133); 1683/4 inventory (PLYM SCRAP p. 40); for further information see also MA PIONEERS p. 488, GEN ADV 1:21, SCITUATE BY DEANE p. 190, DUXBURY BY WINSOR p. 346, PN&Q 2:99

WETHERELL/WITHERELL con't

WILLIAM Sr. of Taunton; 1691 Bristol Co. will mentions unnamed wife and appoints sons William and John executors (BRISTOL CO PR 1:50 or NEHGR 62:179-180); for further information see also SAVAGE 4:492

WEYMOUTH see WAYMOUTH

WHEATON

SAMUEL of Swansea; 1683 inventory sworn by his widow Elizabeth Wheaton (PLYM SCRAP p. 34 or PLYM COL PR 4:2:122); incomplete original 1683/4 bond of administratrix (PLYM SCRAP p. 36); 1683/4 bond of administratrix (PLYM COL RECS 6:124); for further information see also SAVAGE 4:495

WHETSTONE/WHESTON

JOHN of Scituate; 1664 bond of widow Susanna Wheston and Joseph Wheston as administrators with Edward Jenkins as surety, and bond of Joseph for sale of land (PLYM SCRAP pp. 37-38, 48-49); settlements and permission to sell land (PLYM COL RECS 4:75-76, 114); for further information see also SCITUATE BY DEANE p. 380, MA PIONEERS p. 491

JOSEPH, probably of Scituate; son of John above; died at Boston; 1666 guardianship of brother (PLYM COL RECS 4:139); inventory (SUFFOLK CO PROBATE OLD SERIES 5:13)

WHITE

GOWIN of Scituate; 1664 inventory (MD 16:126 or PLYM SCRAP p. 33); administration granted to Timothy and Joseph White (PLYM COL RECS 4:81); bond of administrators (PLYM CO PR #22555 1/2); for further information see also MA PIONEERS p. 492, PLYM COL MARR p. 49, SCITUATE BY DEANE p. 382, TAG 17:198-199

SILVANUS of Scituate; grandson of Pilgrim William White; 1688 administration, with inventory sworn by his widow Deborah White (PN&Q 4:123 or GEN ADV 1:20); for further information see also MF 1:110

WHITNEY/WHITON

THOMAS of Plymouth; 1673 will, exhibited 1673/4, names wife Patience (PLYM COL PR 3:2:6-7); for further information see also MA PIONEERS p. 495, NEHGR 123:228 [date of his will is given incorrectly]

WIATT see WYATT

WILBOR

JOSEPH of Taunton; 1691 Bristol Co. will names daughter Anna Wilbor executrix (GEN ADV 4:59); for further information see also SAVAGE 4:544

SAMUEL of Taunton; 1656 will names wife Elizabeth (MD 14:150); for further information see also MA PIONEERS p. 497

WILLETT

THOMAS of Swansea; former New York Colony Governor; 1671 will, sworn 1674, names sons James, Hezekiah, Andrew and Samuel executors (MD 26:80); inventory (MD 33:35); for further information see also MA PIONEERS p. 499, SAVAGE 4:557

WILLIAMS

EDWARD of Scituate; 1671 administration granted to John Williams (PLYM COL RECS 5:81, 89, 102, 138, 7:176); for further information see also MA PIONEERS p. 499

JOHN Sr. of Scituate; 1667 will, probated 1667/8, names daughter Mary Dodson executrix (MD 17:109); administration (PLYM COL RECS 4:175); for further information see also MA PIONEERS p. 499, PLYM COL RECS 7:146, SCITUATE BY DEANE p. 385, SCITUATE BY PRATT p. 353

WILLIAMSON

TIMOTHY Sr. of Marshfield; not the "Mr. Williamson" of 1621; 1676 will mentions unnamed wife, inventory sworn by widow Mary Williamson (PLYM COL PR 3:2:20-21); guardianship for son (PLYM COL RECS 6:97); 1690 settlement and guardians for children (PLYM CO CT RECS 1:206-7); for further information see also MA PIONEERS p. 501, NEHGR 81:72ff, NGSQ (June 1983)

WILLIAMSON con't

TIMOTHY of Marshfield; son of Timothy above; 1682 settlement to unnamed siblings (PLYM COL PR 4:2:4); for further information see also MA PIONEERS p. 502, NEHGR 81:78ff, NGSQ (June 1983)

WILLIS

NATHANIEL Sr. of Bridgewater; 1686 administration granted to son Elkanan and mention of unnamed widow (PN&Q 4:2 or GEN ADV 1:17); for further information see also MA PIONEERS p. 502, CAPE COD HIST 2:55

RICHARD of Plymouth; 1678 original inventory [very damaged] (PLYM SCRAP p. 50); inventory sworn by widow Patience Willis (PLYM COL PR 4:1:13); 1678/9 settlement (PLYM COL RECS 6:4); for further information see also TAG 38:235, SAVAGE 4:577, PLYM TR 1:156, 158

WILLS

ROWLAND of Scituate; not a descendant of William Wills; 1689 nuncupative will bequeaths all to James Briggs (PN&Q 5:115 or GEN ADV 1:114); for further information see also SCITUATE BY DEANE p. 384

WILLIAM of Scituate; 1683 will, sworn 1688, names wife Luce (PN&Q 5:14 or GEN ADV 1:42); for further information see also MA PIONEERS p. 503, SCITUATE BY DEANE p. 384

WINCHESTER

ALEXANDER of Rehoboth; 1647 will, exhibited 1648, appoints unnamed wife executrix (MD 9:30); arrangements for children (PLYM COL RECS 2:126, 136, 169); settlement (PLYM COL RECS 3:120, 142); for further information see also MA PIONEERS p. 505

WING

DANIEL of Sandwich; 1658/9 testimony re settling estate on unnamed children (PLYM COL RECS 3:157); inventory sworn by John and Steven Winge (MD 14:230); for further information see also MA PIONEERS p. 506 (see also entry under Deborah), CAPE COD HIST 2:100

JOHN Jr. of Yarmouth; son of John; 1683 settlement with inventory sworn by his widow Mary Wing (PLYM COL PR 4:2:47); for further information see also SAVAGE 4:594

WINSLOW

EDWARD of Marshfield; Plymouth Colony Governor; came on the ship Mayflower; married Susanna (-----) White, widow of Pilgrim William White; 1654 Prerogative Court of Canterbury, England, will, he "of London," mentions unnamed wife (MD 4:1 or MAY RDR p. 223 or WATERS 1:179 or PCC Aylett 377 [England]); for further information see also MQ 28:2:27, FAMS OF PILGRIMS, MF 1:95-99, MD 5:224, 8:100, NEHGR 122:175, 124:182, TAG 41:168, 42:52, 43:42, NGSQ 63:295, MAY RDR p. 410, SCITUATE BY DEANE p. 388, BRIDGEWATER BY MITCHELL p. 409, AMERICAN COLONISTS BY COLDHAM p. 65

JONATHAN of Marshfield; son of Josiah Sr.; 1676 administration granted to Ruth Winslow (PLYM COL RECS 5:217); 1676 inventory (PLYM COL PR 3:2:11); for further information see also MA PIONEERS p. 508, SAVAGE 4:601

JOSIAH Sr. of Marshfield; brother of Pilgrim Edward Winslow; 1673 will, exhibited 1674, names wife Margaret (MD 34:33); 1674/5 part of will declared void (PLYM COL RECS 5:159-160); for further information see also MA PIONEERS p. 508

JOSIAH Esq. of Marshfield; Plymouth Colony Governor and son of Pilgrim Edward Winslow; 1675 will, sworn 1680/1, names wife Penelope (MD 5:82 or MAY RDR p. 387); for further information see also MD 5:82, FAMS OF PILGRIMS, PLYM COL RECS 6:55, 299, BRIDGEWATER BY MITCHELL p. 410, EARLY REHOBOTH 3:12-13

KENELM Sr. of Marshfield; brother of Pilgrim Edward Winslow; 1672 will names wife Eleanor (MD 24:41); for further information see also MA PIONEERS p. 508, TAG 55:213, SCITUATE BY DEANE p. 389

WINTER

CHRISTOPHER of Scituate; 1680 will, sworn 1683/4, names daughter Martha Huett executrix (PLYM COL PR 4:2:61-62); for further information see also MA PIONEERS p. 508, SCITUATE BY DEANE p. 387

WITHERELL see WETHERELL

WIXAM

ROBERT of Eastham; 1686 Barnstable Co. will names wife Alice (MD 2:177); for further information see also MA PIONEERS p. 496 (under Wickson)

WOOD see also ATWOOD

BENJAMIN of Middleboro; 1690 nuncupative will names brother James Wood alias Atwood (MD 30:69 or GEN ADV 1:116); for further information see also MIDDLEBORO BY WESTON p. 625

HENRY of Middleboro; 1670 inventory sworn by widow Abigail Wood (MD 19:60); inventory (PLYM COL RECS 5:142); administration and guardians (PLYM COL RECS 5:50); 1674 settlement (PLYM COL LR 4:27); for further information see also MA PIONEERS p. 511, MIDDLEBORO BY WESTON p. 61

JOHN of Middleboro; son of Henry Wood alias Atwood; 1673 nuncupative will names eldest brother Samuel Wood (MD 24:133, 135); bond of administrator Samuel Wood alias Atwood (PLYM SCRAP pp. 111-112); for further information see also MIDDLEBORO BY WESTON p. 62

JOHN Jr. of Plymouth; son of John Sr.; 1675/6 division to his brother Nathaniel and others (PLYM COL RECS 5:188), inventory (PLYM COL PR 3:1:178)

JOHN Sr. of Plymouth; 1675 will, exhibited 1675/6, names wife Sarah (PLYM COL PR 3:1:155); 1676 bond of administratrix of estate of John Wood alias Atwood (PLYM SCRAP p. 124); administration (PLYM COL RECS 5:188); 1685 deed of heirs (PLYM COL RECS 6:161-163); for further information see also MA PIONEERS p. 511

JONATHAN of Plymouth; son of Henry; 1675 nuncupative will bequeaths to unnamed siblings (PLYM COL PR 3:1:170-171); 1675/6 administration granted to Samuel and David (PLYM COL RECS 5:189); for further information see also PLYM COL RECS 8:8, SAVAGE 4:626 (under Henry Wood)

WOODFIELD

ESTHER of Scituate; widow of John; 1672 will names Henry Ewell executor (MD 19:62); for further information see also MA PIONEERS p. 512

JOHN of Scituate; 1669 will names wife Hester (MD 17:156); for further information see also MA PIONEERS p. 512, SCITUATE BY DEANE p. 391

WOODWARD

WALTER of Scituate; 1685 will, sworn 1685/6, names eldest son Thomas and others (PLYM COL LR 5:382); for further information see also ME HGR 7:23, MA PIONEERS p. 514, SCITUATE BY DEANE p. 391 (under Woodworth)

WORDEN

MARY of Yarmouth, widow; 1686 Barnstable Co. will, proved 1687, names son-in-law John Burge executor (MD 3:201-202)

PETER the elder of Yarmouth; 1638 will names son Peter executor (MD 3:75); will sworn 1638/9 (PLYM COL RECS 1:117); for further information see also MA PIONEERS p. 515

PETER of Yarmouth; son of Peter; 1679 will with codicil, proved 1680/1, names wife Mary (PLYM COL PR 4:1:72-75); for further information see also MA PIONEERS p. 515, YARMOUTH BY SWIFT p. 69

WORMALL

JOSEPH of Scituate; 1661 will, probated 1662, names wife Meriam (MD 17:217); administration, bond re portion of estate (PLYM COL RECS 4:16, 75); for further information see also MA PIONEERS p. 515, DUXBURY BY WINSOR p. 347

WRIGHT

ISAAC of Plymouth; grandson of Pilgrim Francis Cooke; undated settlement names his father Richard Wright (MD 24:86); 1676 settlement (PLYM COL RECS 5:200); for further information see also FAMS OF PILGRIMS (Cooke family)

WRIGHT con't

JOHN of Plymouth; grandson of Pilgrim Francis Cooke; 1675 will, exhibited 1676, names his father Richard Wright (MD 24:84); 1676 settlement (PLYM COL RECS 5:200); for further information see also MA PIONEERS p. 516, FAMS OF PILGRIMS (Cooke family)

RICHARD of Plymouth; married Hester Cooke, daughter of Pilgrim Francis Cooke; 1691 will names son Adam and daughters Mary Price and Esther Wright executors (MD 4:165 or GEN ADV 2:89); for further information see also FAMS OF PILGRIMS (Cooke family), MA PIONEERS p. 516, MD 24:85

WILLIAM of Plymouth; came on the ship Fortune; 1633 will names wife Priscilla (MD 1:200); for further information see also MF 1:50-51, MA PIONEERS p. 517

WYATT/WIATT

JAMES of Taunton; 1664 inventory sworn by widow Mary Wyatt (MD 16:26); inquest (PLYM COL RECS 4:70-71); for further information see also MA PIONEERS p. 517, PLYM COL RECS 5:154, 157, 272

JAMES of Taunton; 1685 administration granted to Thomas Gilbert (PLYM COL RECS 6:177)

MARY of Taunton, widow; 1679/80 will, sworn 1685, bequeaths all to Hannah, daughter of Thomas Gilbert of Taunton (PLYM COL LR 5:363); will sworn (PLYM COL RECS 6:176)

YATES/YEATES

JOHN of Eastham; 1651 administration granted to Mary Yates (PLYM COL RECS 2:170); for further information see also MA PIONEERS p. 518

JOHN of Eastham; 1682 settlement, with administration granted to widow Deborah Yeates (PLYM COL RECS 6:90-91); inventory (PLYM COL PR 4:1:1b, 2b, 4:2:118)

YEATES see YATES

YOUNG

GEORGE of Scituate; 1672 inventory sworn by widow Hannah Young (MD 19:164); for further information see also MD 2:34, SCITUATE BY DEANE p. 393, TAG 32:194

JOHN Sr. of Eastham; 1688/9 Barnstable Co. will, proved 1691, names wife Abigail (MD 12:39); for further information see also MA PIONEERS p. 518, PLYM COL MARR p. 52, NGSQ (June 1983)

INDEX TO OTHER NAMES IN THE PROBATE GUIDE

MORE THAN 100 people mentioned within the entries in the Guide have surnames other than those of the decedents. This is a cross index to the other names.

ALDEN
  John
    see Paybody, John
    see Seabury, John
ALLEN
  John
    see Chapell, Robert
    see Nicolls, James
    see Piddell, William
ALLERTON
  Isaac
    see Cushman, Thomas
    see Godbertson, Godbert
  Mary
    see Cushman, Thomas
BACON
  Nathaniel
    see Gilpin, Anthony
  Samuel
    see Foxwell, Richard
BANGS
  Apphia
    see Knowles, John
BARTLETT
  Lydia
    see Barnabey, James
BARTLETT con't
  Mary
    see Foster, Richard
  Rebecca
    see Harlow, William
BATTER
  Edward
    see Jones, Robert
BAXTER
  Mr.
    see Tooto
  Temperance
    see Sturgis, Edward
  Thomas
    see Sturgis, Edward
BEARE
  Richard
    see Granger, John
BEARS
  Elizabeth (Billington)
    see Bulloke, Richard
BENJAMIN
  Joseph
    see Clark, William
BILLINGTON
  Dorcas
    see May, Edward

BILLINGTON con't
  Elizabeth
    see Beere, Robert
    see Bulloke, Richard
  John
    see Beere, Robert
    see Bulloke, Richard
    see Eaton, Samuel
    see May, Edward
  Martha
    see Eaton, Samuel
BISHOP
  Alice
    see Clark, Martha
  Richard
    see Clark, Martha
BLAGROVE
  Nathaniel
    see Hayman, Nathan
BLISS
  Jonathan
    see Harmer, Ephraim
BOSWORTH
  Jonathan
    see Cobley, John
    see Peck(e), Nathaniel
BOURNE see also BURNE
  Richard
    see Numacke, Nanquit
BRADFORD
  William
    see Palmer, William
BREWSTER
  Jonathan
    see Evans, Thomas
  Sarah
    see Bartlett, Benjamin
  William
    see Bartlett, Benjamin
    see James, John
    see Mayo, Nathaniel
BRIGGS
  Constant (-----)
    see Fobes, John
BRIGGS con't
  James
    see Wills, Rowland
  Samuel
    see Sanders, Henry
BROWN(E)
  James
    see Howland, Elizabeth
  John
    see Rogers, Hannah
  Mary
    see Tinkham, Ephraim
  Mr.
    see Smith, Francis
    see Smith, Samuel
  Peter
    see Snow, James
    see Tinkham, Ephraim
BULLOCK
  Elizabeth (Billington)
    see Beere, Robert
BURGE
  John
    see Worden, Mary
BURNE see also BOURNE
  John
    see Drayton, Henry
  Thomas
    see Launder(s), William
CANN
  John
    see Bourne, John
CHANDLER
  Martha
    see Bundey, John
  Sarah
    see Leonard, Solomon
CHAPMAN
  Isaac
    see Wells, Margaret
CHILTON
  James
    see Bundey, John
    see Gray, Edward
    see Leonard, Solomon

CHIPMAN
  John
    see Bursley, John
CHURCHILL
  John
    see Rickard, Hannah
  Joseph
    see Rickard, Hannah
CLARKE
  Martha
    see Nash, Samuel
COBB
  John
    see Hurst, Gartherew
COLE
  Hugh
    see Foxwell, Richard
COLLIER
  William
    see Partridge, Ralph
CONKKEQUID see Quonnukquosh
COOKE
  Elizabeth (Dean)
    see Dean, Steven
  Francis
    see Mitchell, Experience
    see Washbourne, Benjamin
    see Washbourne, John
    see Wright, Isaac
    see Wright, John
    see Wright, Richard
  Hester
    see Wright, Richard
  Jane
    see Mitchell, Experience
  Josias
    see Dean, Steven
CORPS
  John
    see Brown, William
CUDWORTH
  Major
    see Lothrop, John
CURTICE
  John
    see Chambers, Richarden
DARBY
  Mathew
    see Turner, John
DELANO
  Esther
    see Samson, Samuel
DEVELL
  William
    see Hazell, John
DIMACKE
  Mistress
    see Turner, John
DOANE/DONE
  John
    see Harding, Martha
DODSON
  Mary
    see Williams, John
DOTY
  Desire
    see Holmes, Israel
    see Sherman, William
  Edward
    see Holmes, Israel
    see Phillips, Faith
    see Sherman, William
EATON
  Francis
    see Ramsden, Joseph
  Rachel
    see Ramdsen, Joseph
EDDENTON
  Edward
    see Granger, Thomas
EDY
  Zacherya
    see Jones, Robert
ELLIS
  Elizabeth (Freeman)
    see Freeman, Edmond
ERCEMAS see Quonnukquosh
ESTERBROKE
  Thomas
    see Jones, Robert

EVANS
Ann
see Crow, William
EWELL
Henry
see Woodfield, Esther
EWER
Thomas
see Huckens, Thomas
FISH
Sissillie [Cecily?]
see Rollocke, Robert
FITCH
John
see Sutton, Julian
FLINT
Margery
see Newman, Joanna
FRENCH
John
see Kingsley, John
Richard
see Beare, Richard
FULLER
Elizabeth
see Rowley, Henry
Matthew
see Rowley, Henry
GILBERT
Hannah
see Wyatt, Mary
Thomas
see Wyatt, James
see Wyatt, Mary
GLADDING
John
see Hinton, John
Susanna
see Hinton, John
GLASS
James
see Pontus, William
GORHAM
James
see Tooto
GORHAM con't
Temperance
see Sturgis, Edward
HALL
Samuel
see Green, Henry
HARDING
John
see Kempton, Manasses
HARRISON
Henry
see Martin, John
Katharine
see Martin, John
HATHERLEY
Timothy
see Lincks, Phillip
see Granger, Thomas
HATHWAY
John
see MacKenney, Daniel
HAWARD
John
see Husey, Robert
HAWKINS
Job
see Holmes, William
HAWXSE
Lodowick
see Chadwell, Richard
HAYWARD see HAWARD
HEWET/HUETT
Martha
see Winter, Christopher
HILL
Ebenezer
see Bayley, Guido
HINCKLEY
Thomas
see Cobb, Sarah
HOBART
Gershom
see Rogers, Hannah
Nehemiah
see Rogers, Hannah

HODGIS
William
see Gilpin, Anthony
HOLMES
Israel
see Sherman, William
HOPKINS
Constance
see Snow, Nicholas
Stephen
see Mayo, William
see Snow, Jabez
see Snow, Nicholas
HOSKENS
William
see Riffe, Peter
HOWARD see HAWARD
HOWES
Thomas
see Hallett, Samuel
HOWLAND
Arthur
see Damon, John Sr.
Desire
see Gorham, Desire
see Gorham, John
John
see Evans, Thomas
see Gorham, Desire
see Gorham, John
see Lee, Mary
see Sturgis, Edward
Joseph
see Southworth, Thomas
HUCKENS/HUCKINS
Thomas
see Turner, John
see Ewer, Thomas
HUDSON
Ann
see Russell, George
John
see Russell, George
HUNT
Lt.
see Smith, Henry
Peter
see Fallowell, Jonathan
IRISH
John
see Wallis, Henry
JENKINS
Edward
see Whetstone, John
see Whetstone, Joseph
Joell
see Jones, Robert
Mary
see Lewis, Joseph
KENT
Joseph
see Cahoon, William
KINGSLEY
John
see Jones, Samuel
LAMBERT
Joshua
see Jackson, Hugh
LANNE
Job
see Howell, Thomas
LAPHAM
Thomas
see Cushman, James
LATHAM
Robert
see Walker, John
LAYTHORP(E) see LOTHROP
LEONARD
James
see Billington, Thomas
Thomas
see MacKenney, Daniel
LINCOLN
Thomas
see Stacy, Richard

LOTHROP
Barnabas
see Chase, William
see Muckroy, John
Hannah (-----)
see Fuller, Dr. John
Mr.
see Mathewes, James
LUMBART/LUMBERT
Barnard
see More, Cornelius
Caleb
see Cahoon, William
Jabez
see Darbey, Mathew
MARSHALL
Esther
see Bell, James
MAYO
Samuel
see Hallett, Samuel
MILLER
John
see Wells, Margaret
Jone
see Coggen, Thomas
Obadiah
see Coggen, Thomas
MITCHELL
Elizabeth
see Washbourne, John
MOREY
Jonathan
see Foster, Benjamin
NASH
Esther
see Samson, Samuel
NELSON
John
see Barnabey, James
NEWMAN
Samuel
see Sears, Robert
NUMACKE
William
see Pompaquine
ORMSBE(Y)
John
see Martin, Johanna
Thomas
see Sears, Robert
PABODIE
Martha
see Seabury, John
PAINE
Nathaniel
see Smith, Henry
see Sutton, John
PALSGRAVE
Mrs.
see Alcock, John
PARKER
Robert
see Shaw, Thomas
William
see Paine, Alice
PEABODY see PABODIE
PEAKES
Judith (Dennis)
see Dennis, William
William
see Dennis, William
PECKE
Nicholas
see Colby, James
PEIRSE
Joseph
see Bartlett, Moses
PERREY see PERRY
PERRIN
John
see Ormsbey, Jacob
PERRY
Edward
see Freeman, Edmond
Ezra
see Burg, Thomas
PINCIN
Thomas
see Rickard, Thomas

PRATT
Joshua
see Lanckford, Richard
PRENCE
Hannah
see Mayo, Nathaniel
Thomas
see Collier, William
PRICE
Mary
see Wright, Richard
PRIEST
Degory
see Combe, Francis
see Godbertson, Godbert
REIFE
Peter
see Miller alias Hodgis
RICE see RYCE
RICHARDSON
Amos
see Smith, James
RICHMOND
John
see Combe, Francis
RIDER
John
see Hore, Elizabeth
RING
Elizabeth
see Mayo, William
ROBINSON
Increase
see Paine, John
ROES
Allis
see Pickles, Jonas
Thomas
see Pickles, Jonas
ROGERS
Hannah
see Terry, Thomas
see Tisdale, John Jr.
John
see Briggs, Frances
ROGERS con't
Joseph
see Briggs, Frances
Thomas
see Terry, Thomas
see Tisdale, John Jr.
ROWLEY
Moses
see Palmer, William
RYCE
Lenard
see Pilbeame, James
SHERMAN
William
see Burrowes, Jeremiah
SKIFFE
James
see Green, John
SMITH
John
see Bewitt, George
see Bursley, John
SOULE
George
see Peterson, John
John
see Chandler, Samuel
see Samson, Samuel
SOUTHWORTH
Constant
see Hunt, Edward
see Lindale, Mary
STANLAKE
Lydia
see Barstow, Jeremiah
Richard
see Barstow, Jeremiah
STEVENSON
John
see Blackstone, William
STEWART
Hugh
see Phelps, Thomas
SUTTON
John
see Bucke, John

TAYLOR
Henry
see Hatch, Thomas
Lydia
see Hatch, Thomas
THACHER/THATCHER
Elizabeth
see Partridge, Ralph
John
see Chase, William
Mr.
see Mathewes, James
THAYER
Richard
see Paine, John
THOMAS
Nathaniel
see Hanmer, Joseph
Sarah (Pitney)
see Pitney, James
TILLEY
John
see Howland, Elizabeth
TORLTON
Elizabeth (-----)
see Forster, James
John
see Forster, James
TUBBS
William
see Soane, William
TUPPER
Thomas
see Hampton, Thomas
see Sanders, Henry
TURNER
John
see James, John
Lydia
see James, John
USHER
John
see Waldron, Isaac
VIXON
Robert
see Brewster, Nathaniel
WADSWORTH
Christopher
see Hunt, Edward
WALKER
Peter
see Brown, William
WARREN
Anna
see Little, Thomas
Elizabeth
see Church, Richard
Mary
see Bartlett, Robert
Richard
see Barnabey, James
see Bartlett, Benjamin
see Bartlett, Robert
see Blackwell, John
see Church, Nathaniel
see Church, Richard
see Foster, Benjamin
see Foster, Richard
see Harlow, William
see Little, Thomas
Sarah
see Blackwell, John
WATERMAN
Robert
see Launder(s), William
Widow
see Browning, John
WATSON
George
see Bond, John
see Hicks, Margaret
WEBB
Margaret
see Holmes, William
WHITE
Susanna (-----)
see Winslow, Edward
Timothy
see Combe, Daniel
William
see Winslow, Edward

WHITNEY
Thomas
see Smith, Jeremiah
Winifred
see Smith, Jeremiah
WILBOR
Joseph
see England, William
WILLETT
Thomas
see Martin, Robert
WILLIS
Elizabeth
see Palmer, William
John
see Palmer, William
WILLMARTH/WILLMORE
Thomas
see Bliss, Thomas
WINSLOW
Edward
see Chambers, Robert
see Lanckford, Richard
Josiah Sr.
see Drayton, Henry
Josias
see Burrowes, Jeremiah
Kenelm
see Adams, James
see Drayton, Henry
WINTER
Anne
see Batson, Anne
Christopher
see Hewet, Martha
WITHERELL
William
see Irish, Elias
WOOD
Steven
see Knowles, John
WORTHYLAKE
Peter
see Bird, Thomas

OTHER PUBLISHED PROBATE RECORDS

Following are the names of persons who fall outside the scope of the body of this work, but for whom probate records are published in *The Mayflower Descendant*, *The Genealogical Advertiser*, and *Pilgrim Notes & Queries*.

NOTE: The towns of Barrington, Bristol, Little Compton, Tiverton, and Warren are now part of Rhode Island.

ADAMS

- Joseph Sr., of Braintree, 1694 will PN&Q 2:51
- Joseph, of Braintree, 1733/4 will MD 18:112
- Samuel (Capt.), of Chelmsford, 1692 administration PN&Q 2:50

ALDEN

- Benjamin, of Duxbury, 1741 estate MD 24:78
- David, of Duxbury, 1719 inventory MD 6:239
- Ebenezer, of Middleboro, 1748 estate MD 23:130
- Elizabeth, of Duxbury, 1772 estate MD 24:81
- Hannah, of Duxbury, 1739 will MD 20:14
- Hannah, of Middleboro, 1732 will MD 23:116
- Isaac, of Bridgewater, 1773 will MD 22:189
- Isaac[4] Sr., of Duxbury, 1727 will MD 20:49
- John[3], of Boston, 1727 administration MD 10:82
- John[3], of Boston, 1727 will MD 10:80
- John, of Boston, 1747 will MD 12:75
- John, of Middleboro, 1730 will MD 23:112
- John (Capt.), of Boston, 1701 will & inventory MD 6:193
- John (Col.), of Duxbury, 1739 estate MD 20:12
- Jonathan (Capt.), of Duxbury, 1696/7 settlement & inventory MD 6:174
- Joseph Sr., of Bridgewater, 1696 will & inventory MD 6:71
- Nathaniel, of Boston, 1702 administration MD 10:77
- Nathaniel (Capt.), of Boston, 1740 administration inventory MD 12:72

ALDEN con't
Samuel (Capt.), of Duxbury, 1779 will MD 20:76
William (Capt.), of Boston, 1728 will MD 10:79
Zachariah, of Boston, 1709 administration MD 10:79
ALLEN
Francis, of Sandwich, 1696 inventory MD 32:83
Ralph, of Sandwich, 1691 will MD 32:166
Thomas, of Barnstable, 1696/7 inventory MD 31:185
William, of Sandwich, 1697/8 will MD 32:26
ALLERTON
Isaac, of New Haven CT, 1659 will & inventory MD 2:155
Isaac, of Westmoreland VA, 1702 will MD 7:173
ALLYN see ALLEN
ARNOLD
Samuel, of Marshfield, 1693 will GEN ADV 3:94
Seth, of Duxbury, 1715 will MD 25:36
ATKINS
Henry, of Eastham, 1700 will MD 34:131
AVERY
John, of Truro, 1754 will MD 22:163
BACON
Sarah, of Plymouth, 1749 estate MD 25:14
BAKER
Francis, of Yarmouth, 1692/3 will MD 31:107
Kenelm, of Marshfield, 1712 will MD 24:27
Nathaniel, of Yarmouth, 1691/2 inventory MD 14:117
BARKER
Francis Jr., of Duxbury, 1694 administration GEN ADV 3:111
Robert Sr., of Duxbury, 1689 will MD 31:102, GEN ADV 2:106
BARLOW
Jane, of Sandwich, 1693 will MD 19:44
BARNES
Jonathan, of Plymouth, 1714 will MD 12:256
BARRELL
Lydia, of Scituate, 1714 will MD 19:147
BARROWS
John, of Plymouth, 1691/2 will MD 31:159, GEN ADV 3:26
BARTLETT
Benjamin, of Duxbury, 1717 will MD 18:178
Ichabod, of Duxbury, 1716 estate MD 25:16
James, of Plymouth, 1724 estate MD 21:131
John, of Plymouth, 1772 will MD 20:126
Joseph Jr., of Plymouth, 1703 estate MD 19:72

BARTLETT con't
  Joseph, of Plymouth, 1711 inventory MD 12:14
  Robert, of Plymouth, 1717/8 estate MD 20:118
  Thomas, of Plymouth, 1758 will MD 21:167
BASS
  John, of Braintree, 1716 will & inventory MD 4:202
  John, of Braintree, 1723 will MD 18:105
  Joseph, of Boston, 1732 will MD 18:107
BAXTER
  Elizabeth, of Yarmouth, 1741 will MD 13:248
  Shubael, of Yarmouth, 1738 will MD 13:247
  Temperance, of Yarmouth, 1714/5 administration MD 12:221
  Thomas, of Yarmouth, 1713 will MD 12:218
BELL
  John, of Yarmouth, 1700 estate MD 34:130
BENNETT
  Peter (Capt.), of Middleboro, 1749 will MD 21:172
  Priscilla, of Middleboro, 1749 estate MD 21:175
BESBEY
  Hopestill, of Marshfield, 1695/6 administration GEN ADV 4:92
BONNEY
  Thomas Sr., of Duxbury, 1688/9 will sworn 1693 MD 34:182, GEN ADV 3:89
BOSWORTH/BOZWORTH
  David, of Halifax, 1740 will MD 27:80
BOURN(E)
  Meletiah, of Sandwich, 1742 will MD 19:37
  Mercy, of Barnstable, 1781 will MD 19:41
  Silvanus, of Barnstable, 1763 will MD 19:40
BOWEN
  Obadiah, of Swansea, 1708 will & inventory MD 18:204
  Thomas, of Swansea, 1730 will MD 18:210
BOZWORTH see BOSWORTH
BRADFORD
  David, of Kingston, 1730 estate MD 23:183
  Elizabeth, of Plymouth, 1778 estate MD 25:28
  Ephraim (Lt.), of Kingston, 1741 will MD 21:190
  Jael, of Kingston, 1729 will MD 16:114
  John Jr., of Plymouth, 1724 will MD 16:119
  John (Major), of Kingston, 1732 will MD 20:134
  Joseph, of Plymouth, 1712 will MD 5:217
  Samuel, of Duxbury, 1713/4 will MD 16:116
  Samuel (Lt.), of Plympton, 1729/30 will MD 23:14

BRADFORD con't
William (Major), of Plymouth, 1703 will & inventory MD 4:143
William Jr., of Kingston, 1728 estate MD 23:156
William, of Kingston, 1730 estate MD 24:155
BRANCH
Experience, of Marshfield, 1697 inventory MD 32:118
John, of Marshfield, 1699 will MD 32:123
Remember, of Marshfield, 1711 estate MD 32:125
BREWSTER
Wrestling, of Duxbury, 1696/7 inventory MD 20:113
Wrestling, of Kingston, 1765 will MD 20:115
BRIGGS
Cornelius, of Scituate, 1693 will GEN ADV 4:88
BROWN(E)
James, of Swansea, 1694 will & inventory MD 7:163
James (Lt.), of Swansea, 1717 will & inventory MD 17:193
Margaret, of Barrington, 1733/4 will MD 17:197
Noah, of Attleboro, 1776 estate MD 21:129
William, of Eastham, 1685 will, 1694 inventory MD 22:186
William, of Swansea, 1731/2 estate MD 20:178
BRUNING
Joseph, of Boston, 1691 estate MD 20:40
BUCK
Isaac (Lt.), of Scituate, 1695 administration GEN ADV 4:90
John, of Scituate, 1697 will MD 14:128
BURDEN
William, of Middleboro, 1692/3 administration GEN ADV 3:91
BURGE
Joseph, of Rochester, 1695 will MD 27:35
CADMAN
George, of Dartmouth, 1718 will MD 22:3
Hannah, of Dartmouth, 1748/9 will MD 22:5
CARSELY
John, of Barnstable, 1693 inventory MD 22:185
CARY
Jonathan, of Bridgewater, 1695 administration GEN ADV 4:91
CHANDLER
Elizabeth, of Duxbury, 1728 will MD 12:111
Joseph, of Duxbury, 1721 will MD 14:69

CHIPMAN
John (Elder), of Sandwich, 1702 will & inventory MD 3:181
John, of Beverly, 1769 will MD 29:149
Ruth, of Sandwich, 1710 will MD 3:185
Samuel, of Barnstable, 1722 will MD 16:65
Sarah, of Barnstable, 1733 will MD 16:67

CHURCH
Benjamin (Col.), of Little Compton, 1717/8 inventory MD 7:100
Benjamin, of Boston, 1780 will & inventory MD 8:54; 1781 administration MD 10:119
Edward (Capt.), of Bristol, 1706 inventory MD 7:135
Joseph, of Little Compton, 1710/1 will MD 22:23
Richard, of Hingham, 1668 will & inventory MD 5:118
Richard, of Scituate, 1703 estate MD 22:153

CLAPP
Priscilla, of Scituate, 1833 will MD 22:20
William, of Scituate, 1804 will MD 22:17

COBB
James (Sgt.), of Barnstable, 1695 inventory MD 31:33
John Sr., of Middleboro, 1727 will MD 24:36

COBHAM
Josiah, of Boston, 1697/8 will MD 20:40

COLE
Daniel, of Eastham, 1694 estate MD 23:67

COLEMAN
Joseph, of Scituate, 1694 estate GEN ADV 3:112, 4:25

COLLAMER
Anthony (Capt.), of Scituate, 1694 administration GEN ADV 4:89

COOK(E)
Caleb, of Plymouth, 1721 will MD 15:136
Caleb, of Plymouth, 1724 estate MD 16:148
Francis, of Plympton, 1724 estate MD 16:149
Francis, of Kingston, 1732 will & inventory 18:147
Hannah, of Kingston, 1760 estate MD 17:57
Jacob, of Kingston, 1728 will MD 21:43
Jane, of Kingston, 1736 will MD 15:139
John, of Dartmouth, 1694 will & inventory MD 3:33 (he came on the *Mayflower*)
John Sr., of Kingston, 1741 will MD 17:56
Josiah, of Eastham, 1727 will MD 5:185
Robert, of Kingston, 1731 will MD 16:150
Robert Jr., of Kingston, 1743 estate MD 17:58

CROCKER
  Daniel, of Marshfield, 1693 administration GEN ADV 3:91
  Eleazer, of Barnstable, 1723 inventory MD 18:159
  Jabez, of Barnstable, 1700 estate MD 34:56
  Josiah, of Barnstable, 1698/9 will MD 33:139
  William (Deacon), of Barnstable, 1692 will MD 18:58
CURTICE
  Richard, of Scituate, 1692 will GEN ADV 3:110
CUSHMAN
  Elkanah (Deacon), of Plympton, 1725 will MD 5:20
  Isaac (Rev.), of Plympton, 1727 will MD 17:139
  Josiah (Lt.), of Plympton, 1742 will MD 21:102
DAMON
  Daniel, of Scituate, 1695/6 will GEN ADV 4:91, 92
DELANO
  Benoni (Dr.), of Duxbury, 1738 estate MD 20:33
  Jonathan, of Dartmouth, 1720 will MD 23:148
  Thomas Sr., of Duxbury, 1722 will & inventory MD 6:22
DEXTER
  James, of Rochester, 1697 will MD 33:138
  William, of Barnstable, 1694 estate MD 23:64
DIMMOCK/DIMMUCK
  Thomas (Capt.), of Barnstable, 1698 inventory MD 33:137
DOANE
  Ephraim, of Eastham, 1699 will MD 34:56
DODSON
  Mary, no town given, 1695 will GEN ADV 4:92
DOGGET
  Thomas, of Marshfield, 1689 will GEN ADV 3:90
DOTEN/DOTEY
  Elisha, of Plymouth, 1753 will MD 19:178
  Hannah, of Plymouth, 1754 will MD 20:30
  Isaac, of Plymouth, 1724 estate, MD 25:165
  James, of Plymouth, 1785 will MD 19:179
  John Sr., of Plymouth, 1701 will & inventory MD 6:77; 1701 guardianships MD 33:114, GEN ADV 3:27
  John, of Plympton, 1746 will MD 20:28
  Neriah, of Plymouth, 1738 will MD 25:173
  Stephen, of Plymouth, 1802 estate MD 19:183
DREW
  John, of Halifax, 1742 will & inventory MD 7:114
DUNHAM
  John, of Plymouth, 1691/2 will MD 31:160, GEN ADV 3:27
  John, of Barnstable, 1696/7 inventory MD 31:108

DWELLEY
Richard, of Scituate, 1692 inventory MD 34:182 GEN ADV 3:89
EAMES
Mark (Lt.), of Marshfield, 1693 will GEN ADV 3:93, 4:92
EARLE
John, of Tiverton, 1718/9 will MD 17:61
Mary, of Tiverton, 1731/2 settlement MD 17:62
Mary, of Tiverton, 1735 will MD 17:63
EATON
Samuel, of Middleboro, 1724 administration MD 12:227
Samuel, of Middleboro, 1815 will MD 18:125
EDDY
Obadiah, of Middleboro, 1722 will PN&Q 5:104
EDSON
Samuel Sr., of Bridgewater, 1688/9 will, 1692 inventory MD 34:181, GEN ADV 3:28
FAXON
Sarah, of Braintree, 1694 will & inventory MD 7:182
Thomas, of Braintree, 1680 inventory MD 7:45
FESSENDEN
Benjamin, of Sandwich, 1783 will MD 20:59
Sarah, of Sandwich, 1793 will MD 20:60
FIELD
George, of Sandwich, 1693 estate MD 22:185
FINNEY see PHINNEY
FISH
Nathaniel, of Sandwich, 1693/4 inventory MD 23:66
Samuel, of Sandwich, 1691/2 will MD 15:77
FORD
John, of Marshfield, 1693 administration GEN ADV 3:93
FOSTER
John, of Plymouth, 1739/40 will MD 24:25
FREEMAN
Edmund (Lt.), of Eastham, 1717/8 settlement MD 8:65
John (Major), of Eastham, 1716 will & inventory MD 5:143
John, of Harwich, 1721 will MD 33:108
Jonathan, of Harwich, 1715 administration MD 13:20
Mercy, of Harwich, 1721 estate MD 33:13
Sarah, of Eastham, 1736/7 will & inventory MD 8:65
Thomas (Deacon), of Harwich, 1715/6 will MD 13:20
Thomas Jr., of Harwich, 1717 inventory MD 13:22

FULLER
John (Dr.), of Barnstable, 1699 estate MD 33:171
Matthias, of Barnstable, 1696 will MD 31:187
Samuel, of Middleboro, 1695 inventory MD 5:65, GEN ADV 4:90
GAGE
Thomas Sr., of Harwich, 1695 will MD 24:63
GANNET
Matthew, no town given, 1694 will GEN ADV 4:89
GAUNT
Israel, of Sandwich, 1697/8 will MD 32:83
Lydia, of Sandwich, 1691 will MD 15:76
GIBBS
Thomas, of Sandwich, 1692/3 inventory MD 18:61
Thomas Sr., of Sandwich, 1725 will, MD 23:124
GILBERT
Nathaniel (Capt.), of Berkley, 1757 will MD 21:117
GLASS
Roger, no town given, 1690 will GEN ADV 3:89
GORHAM
Jabez, of Bristol, 1724/5 will MD 17:67
Jabez, of Bristol, 1745 estate MD 17:69
James, of Barnstable, 1707 will MD 13:51
John (Col.), Barnstable, 1716 will MD 13:52
Mary, of Barnstable, 1727 will MD 13:54
Stephen, of Barnstable, 1743 will MD 22:171
GRAY
John, of Kingston, 1728 will MD 21:63
Thomas (Capt.), of Little Compton, 1721 will MD 21:84
Thomas, of Little Compton, 1723 will MD 21:157
GUSHEE
Abraham Jr., of Raynham, 1775 estate MD 21:81
Abraham Sr., of Raynham, 1782 estate MD 21:83
HADAWAY see HATHAWAY
HALL
John Sr., of Yarmouth, 1694 will MD 31:36
Samuel, of Yarmouth, 1693 will MD 22:185
HALLETT
Anna, of Yarmouth, 1684 will, 1694 inventory MD 22:188
HARDING
John, of Eastham, 1697 estate MD 32:81
HARLOW
Samuel, of Plymouth, 1724/5 will MD 20:164
HASKELL
John, of Middleboro, 1706 inventory MD 6:6
Mark, of Rochester, 1699 will MD 34:54

HATCH
Ezekiel, of Rochester, 1765 will MD 22:155
Josiah, of Rochester, 1715 inventory MD 27:98
Samuel Sr., of Scituate, 1728 will & inventory MD 7:29
HATHAWAY
Arthur, of Dartmouth, 1709/10 will MD 16:110
Jethro, of New Bedford, 1798 will MD 17:76
John, of Yarmouth, 1689 will MD 31:185
Thomas, of Dartmouth, 1742 will MD 16:112
HAWES
Edmund, of Yarmouth, 1692 will MD 19:43
John (Capt.), of Yarmouth, 1701 will MD 20:74
HAWKES
Adam, of Lynn, 1671/2 inventory MD 17:225
Adam, of Lynn, 1691 inventory MD 17:227
John, of Lynn, 1694 estate MD 17:228
Moses, of Lynn, 1708 will MD 17:232
HEAIRO
Peter, of Boston, 1743 administration MD 12:74
HIGGINS
Benjamin, of Eastham, 1760 will MD 18:190
HINCKLEY
Samuel, of Barnstable, 1696 will & inventory MD 10:14
Thomas, of Barnstable, 1700 will & inventory MD 5:237
HOBART
Israel, of Scituate, 1729 will MD 18:127
Peter (Rev.), of Hingham, 1678 will MD 19:188
HODGES
Henry Sr., of Taunton, 1717 will MD 21:96
HOLLEY
Joseph, of Barnstable, 1692 settlement MD 16:60
HOLMES
Bathsheba, of Halifax, 1762 will MD 20:167
George, of Plymouth, 1746 will MD 18:232
Joseph Sr., of Kingston, 1733 will MD 20:169
William, of Halifax, 1760 estate MD 20:166
HOPKINS
Caleb, of Truro, 1728 settlement MD 8:240
Caleb, of Truro, 1741 estate MD 16:35
Elisha, of Chatham, 1741/2 will MD 16:36
John, of Harwich, 1738/9 inventory MD 15:177
Joshua, of Eastham, 1734 will MD 15:175
Joshua, of Eastham, 1775 will MD 20:68
Judah, of Harwich, 1747 will MD 15:117
Samuel, of Harwich, 1749 will MD 15:119
Stephen, of Harwich, 1732/3 will MD 15:116

HOWES
Joseph, of Yarmouth, 1694/5 will MD 23:68
Thomas, of Yarmouth, 1700 estate & inventory MD 34:130, 131

HOWLAND
Elizabeth, of Middleboro, 1725 will MD 17:188 (abstract), 219
Isaac, of Middleboro, 1718 will & inventory MD 6:147
Isaac Jr., of Middleboro, 1723/4 estate MD 17:189
Isaac, of Barnstable, 1751 will MD 10:89
Jabez, of Bristol, 1708 will & inventory MD 7:198
Jabez, of Bristol, 1732 estate MD 21:146
Jabez, of Barnstable, 1764 will MD 11:82
John, of Barnstable, 1737/8 will MD 10:87
John, of Barnstable, 1747 will MD 10:88
Joseph, of Duxbury, 1692 inventory MD 34:37, GEN ADV 3:28, 3:92
Joseph (Capt.), of Plymouth, 1703 will & inventory MD 6:86
Mercy, of Barnstable, 1758 will MD 10:87
Seth, of Middleboro, 1729 will MD 21:179
Shubael, of Barnstable, 1737 will MD 10:86
Thomas, of Plymouth, 1739 will MD 27:82
Zaccheus, of Barnstable, 1740/1 inventory & settlement MD 11:32

HUCKINS
Sarah, of Harwich, 1726/7 will MD 10:14

HUNT
Sarah, of Chilmark, 1771 estate MD 28:108
William, of Chilmark, 1760 will MD 28:107

ILLSELY
Abigail, of Portland ME, 1828 & 1836 wills MD 8:234

Indian
Will, of Scituate, 1695 will GEN ADV 4:990

JAMES
John (Capt.), of Scituate, 1744 will MD 20:153

JENKINS
Josiah, of Barnstable, 1749 will MD 22:158
Thomas, of Barnstable, 1737 will MD 22:157

JENNEY
Samuel, of Dartmouth, 1685 will, 1692 inventory MD 33:79, GEN ADV 3:27

JOHNSON
George, of Somerset Co., Maryland, 1680 will GEN ADV 4:50

JONES
  Ralph, of Barnstable, 1691 will MD 15:78
JOYCE
  John, of Yarmouth, 1714 will MD 9:123
KEEN
  Josiah, of Duxbury, 1695 will MD 19:129
  Josiah, of Pembroke, 1728 will MD 19:130
KINGMAN
  Samuel, of Bridgewater, 1740 will MD 31:28
KINGSLEY
  Samuel, of Taunton, 1713 inventory MD 30:16
KNOWLES
  Joshua, of Eastham, 1778 will MD 25:110
LATHAM
  Deliverance, of Bridgewater, 1749 will MD 22:120
  James, of Bridgewater, 1738 will MD 22:118
LATHROP
  Edward, of Bridgewater, 1696 administration, GEN ADV 4:93
LEONARD
  Joseph, of Taunton, 1692 will GEN ADV 4:124
LITTLE
  Barnabas, of Scituate, 1789 will MD 34:172
  Constant, of Marshfield, 1767 will MD 19:172
  David, of Scituate, 1750 will MD 34:151
  Ephraim, of Plymouth, 1712/3 estate MD 34:153
  Ephraim, of Marshfield, 1715 will MD 19:159
  Isaac (Lt.), of Marshfield, 1699 estate MD 24:3
  John, of Marshfield, 1764 will MD 19:166
  Samuel, of Bristol, 1707 will MD 17:83
  Sarah, of Bristol, 1736/7 estate MD 17:85
  Sarah, of Plymouth, 1760 estate MD 34:154
LORING
  Anna, of Duxbury, 1787 will MD 21:126
LUCAS
  Samuel Sr., of Plymouth, 1715 will MD 27:22
MacCALL
  James, of Marshfield, 1693 administration GEN ADV 3:92
MACOMBER
  Onesimus, of Marshfield, 1767 will MD 19:18
  Thomas Jr., of Marshfield, 1749 estate MD 19:17
  Thomas Sr., of Marshfield, 1767 will MD 19:18
MAIHEW
  Mathew, of Tisbury, Wilts, England, 1612 will GEN ADV 4:4

MAKEPEACE
  William, of Taunton, 1736 will MD 21:140
MAVERICK
  Moses, of Marblehead, 1685 will & inventory MD 5:129
MAYHEW see MAIHEW
MENDALL
  John, of Marshfield, 1711 will PN&Q 5:98
MICHELL see MITCHELL
MIDDLECOTT
  Richard, of Boston, 1700 will MD 21:5
  Sarah, of Boston, 1726 estate MD 21:7
MILES
  Anna, of Swansey, 1693/4 inventory GEN ADV 4:123
MILLER
  Francis, of Middleboro, 1746 will MD 25:102
MITCHELL
  Edward, of Bridgewater, 1716/7 will MD 20:140
MORTON
  Ephraim Sr., of Plymouth, 1693 will MD 17:47, GEN ADV 3:109
  Ephraim, of Plymouth, 1717/8 inventory MD 17:51
  Ephraim (Capt.), of Plymouth, 1729/30 estate MD 17:50
  Ephraim, of Plymouth, 1730 will MD 17:49
  John, of Middleboro, 1717/8 will MD 20:91
  Josiah, of Plymouth, 1694 administration GEN ADV 3:112
  Lemuel, of Plymouth, 1779 will MD 27:137
  Thomas, of Plymouth, 1741 will MD 27:136
MOSHER
  Joseph, of Dartmouth, 1743 will MD 30:25
MULLINS
  William, of Braintree, 1673/4 inventory MD 7:37
NELSON
  John, of Plymouth, 1697 will MD 19:191
NEWCOMB
  William, of Sandwich, 1736 estate MD 20:58
NEWLAND
  William, of Sandwich, 1690 will & 1694 inventory MD 24:61, 23:66
NORCUTT
  William, of Marshfield, 1692 will GEN ADV 3:109
OAKMAN
  Tobias, of Marshfield, 1745 will MD 22:36
O'KILLEY/O'KILLIA
  John, of Yarmouth, 1693 estate MD 19:45
  David, of Yarmouth, 1696/7 will MD 32:82

ORCUTT
William, of Bridgewater, 1693 administration GEN ADV 3:110; 1694 agreement GEN ADV 4:89
ORRIS
Nathaniel, of Barnstable, 1696 inventory MD 31:108
OTIS
Job, of Scituate, 1752 willl MD 20:105
Priscilla, of Scituate, 1750 will MD 20:104
PABODIE
William, of Little Compton, 1707 will & inventory MD 6:129
William, of Little Compton, 1743 will MD 23:106
PAINE/PAYNE
John, of Eastham, 1731 will MD 25:116
Joseph (Ensign), of Harwich, 1712 inventory MD 25:124
Samuel, of Eastham, 1712/3 inventory MD 19:93
Thomas, of Eastham, 1705 will MD 15:189
Thomas, of Truro, 1720 will MD 28:162
Tobias, of Boston, 1669 will MD 21:4
PARSIVALL
James (Lt.), of Barnstable, 1691/2 will MD 14:118
PARTRIDGE
George, of Duxbury, 1682 will GEN ADV 4:90
PEABODY see PABODIE
PEARCE
Richard, of Misconcus [Maine], 1720/1 settlement GEN ADV 1:95
PERRY/PERREY
Edward, of Sandwich, 1694 will MD 24:59
William, of Marshfield, 1693 administration GEN ADV 3:91
William, of Marshfield, 1694 administration GEN ADV 3:112
PHILLIPS
John, of Marshfield, 1691 will MD 34:36, GEN ADV 3:28
PHINNEY/FINNEY
Joanna, of Swansea, 1740 estate MD 23:167
John, of Barnstable, 1718 will MD 20:143
John, of Barnstable, 1735 will MD 20:143
Jonathan, of Swansea, 1724 will MD 23:166
Josiah (Lt.), of Plymouth, 1723 will MD 20:98
PINCIN
Thomas, of Scituate, 1689 will GEN ADV 3:112
PRATT
Daniel, of Plympton, 1739 will MD 11:243

PRATT con't
Phineas, of Charlestown, 1677 will & inventory MD 4:137
PRINCE/PRENCE
Mary, of Yarmouth, 1695 inventory MD 6:234
PRYOR
Joseph, of Duxbury, 1692/3 administration GEN ADV 3:89
QUONNUKQUOSH
1681 will MD 22:187
RANDALL
William, of Scituate, 1692 will GEN ADV 3:110
RAUNCE
John, of Scituate, 1694 will GEN ADV 3:112, 4:90
READ
John, of Marshfield, 1694 administration GEN ADV 4:25
William, of Weymouth, 1705 will MD 23:72
RICH
Richard, of Eastham, 1692 inventory MD 16:60, 1697 estate MD 31:186
RICHARDS
Thomas, of Weymouth, 1650 will MD 9:89
Welthian, of Boston, 1679 will MD 9:91
RICHMOND
Ebenezer, of Middleboro, 1729 will MD 21:187
Samuel, of Taunton, 1736 will MD 21:45
Silvester (Col.), of Dartmouth, 1752 will MD 21:13
Silvester (Col.), of Dighton, 1783 estate MD 21:55
Thomas, of Taunton, 1705 inventory MD 9:58
RIDER/RYDER
John, of Yarmouth, 1702/3 will MD 11:54
Samuel, of Yarmouth, 1702 inventory MD 11:54
Samuel, of Plymouth, 1714 will MD 11:185
RING
Andrew, of Plymouth, 1691 will & inventory MD 4:193, GEN ADV 3:92
Eleazer, of Plymouth, 1734/5 will MD 17:152 or 22:39
Eleazer, of Kingston, 1738 will MD 17:153 or 22:161
Samuel, of Kingston, 1768 will MD 22:170
William[4], of Plymouth, 1730 estate MD 17:151 or 22:38
William[3], of Plymouth, 1730 will MD 17:150 or 22:39
ROGERS
John, of Duxbury, 1691 will MD 5:205
John Jr., of Duxbury, 1696 estate MD 20:22
John, of Barrington, 1732 estate & inventory MD 20:5
John, of Harwich, 1739 agreement MD 18:46

ROGERS con't
  Joseph, of Eastham, 1696 inventory MD 11:178
  Joseph Sr, of Eastham, 1713 will MD 11:180
  Joseph, of Eastham, 1746 will MD 15:166
  Judah, of Eastham, 1738/9 will MD 15:165
  Marah, of Rehoboth, 1739 estate MD 20:11
RYDER see RIDER
SAMSON/SAMPSON
  Ebenezer, of Arundell [Maine], 1746 will GEN ADV 4:86
  Elijah, of Duxbury, 1805 estate MD 22:109
  Henry, of Dartmouth, 1750 estate MD 23:42, 1750 administration GEN ADV 4:87
  James, of Dartmouth, 1715/6 will GEN ADV 4:84-85, MD 6:184
  John, of Bristol, 1734 will GEN ADV 4:87
  John, of Duxbury, 1770 estate MD 20:96
  Joseph, of Dartmouth, 1738/9 inventory GEN ADV 4:87, 1738/9 estate MD 23:176
  Josiah, of Plympton, 1730 estate MD 23:162
  Stephen, of Duxbury, 1714/5 administration & settlement MD 6:114
SARGENT
  John Sr., of Malden, 1708 will MD 24:11
SAVILL
  William Sr., of Braintree, 1668 will & inventory MD 7:41
SAWYER
  Sarah, of Wells [Maine], 1734 will GEN ADV 4:86
  Thomas, of Middleboro, 1695 administration GEN ADV 4:90
  William, of Wells [Maine], 1718 will GEN ADV 4:86
SEARS
  Silas (Lt.), of Yarmouth, 1698 inventory MD 32:165
SHELLEY
  Robert, of Barnstable, 1688/9 will MD 18:60
SHERMAN
  Ebenezer, of Marshfield, 1759 will MD 30:167
  Eleazer, of Marshfield, 1723 estate MD 30:166
  William, of Marshfield, 1739 will MD 25:134
SILVESTER
  Joseph & Hannah, 1734 will MD 19:123
SIMMONS
  John, of Duxbury, 1715 estate MD 19:52
  Mercy, of Duxbury, 1728 will & inventory MD 19:53

SMITH
Abiel, of Boston, 1814 will MD 20:108
John, of Chatham, 1717/8 administration MD 12:237
Mary, of Eastham, 1700 inventory MD 12:116
Samuel Jr., of Eastham, 1692 inventory MD 12:113 & 18:60
Samuel Sr., of Eastham, 1697 inventory MD 12:113
Thomas, of Sandwich, 1700 estate MD 34:133
SNOW
Anthony, of Marshfield, 1685 will & inventory MD 5:1, GEN ADV 3:90
Benjamin, of Bridgewater, 1738 will MD 22:99
Jane, of Harwich, 1703 will MD 18:196
John, of Eastham, 1692 inventory MD 12:190
Josiah, of Marshfield, 1692/3 inventory GEN ADV 3:89, 3:111
Mark, of Eastham, 1694 will MD 18:194
Stephen, of Eastham, 1697 will MD 31:39
William, of Bridgewater, 1698/9 will & inventory MD 8:101
William, of Bridgewater, 1726 estate MD 22:48
SOPER
Oliver (Capt.), of Taunton, 1815 will MD 21:10
SOULE
Benjamin, of Plympton, 1729 will MD 25:73
Deborah, of Dartmouth, 1708/9 will & inventory MD 7:217
Esther, of Middleboro, 1792 will MD 19:140
George, of Dartmouth, 1697 will & inventory MD 7:210
James, of Middleboro, 1736 will MD 23:50
James, of Plympton, 1759 estate MD 30:126
James, of Duxbury, 1794 estate MD 20:149
John, of Duxbury, 1707 inventory MD 4:159
John Sr., of Middleboro, 1743 will MD 19:137
Joseph, of Duxbury, 1755 will MD 11:108
Joseph, of Duxbury, 1794 will MD 20:146
Joshua, of Duxbury, 1767 will MD 11:133
Josiah, of Duxbury, 1762 will MD 11:107
Martha, of Middleboro, 1751 will MD 19:138
Mary, of Plympton, 1773 estate MD 30:128
Micah, of Duxbury, 1778 will MD 24:108
Moses, of Duxbury, 1748 estate & inventory MD 18:233
Nathaniel, of Dartmouth, 1699 inventory MD 7:72
Rebecca, of Middleboro, 1746 will MD 23:54
Rebecca, of Middleboro, 1758 will MD 19:139

SOULE con't
Sarah, of Plympton, 1740 estate MD 25:86
Zachariah, of Plympton, 1751 will MD 30:124
SOUTHWORTH/SOUTHERD
Constant, of Tiverton, 1702 will MD 21:25
Edward, of Duxbury, 1719 will MD 18:245
Esther, of Taunton, 1759 will MD 21:75
Hannah, of Duxbury, 1791 estate MD 19:29
Ichabod (Capt.), of Middleboro, 1757 estate MD 21:74
Jedediah, of Duxbury, 1739 estate MD 19:26
John, of Duxbury, 1750 will MD 19:113
Nathaniel Sr. (Lt.), of Middleboro, 1708 will MD 21:26
Priscilla, of Duxbury, 1761 will MD 19:115
Thomas, of Duxbury, 1742 will MD 19:28
SPARROW
John, of Eastham, 1731 will MD 11:231
Jonathan (Capt.), of Eastham, 1706/7 will MD 12:58
Jonathan, of Eastham, 1737 will MD 11:233
Richard, of Eastham, 1727/8 will MD 11:2
SPRAGUE
Anthony, of Hingham, 1716 will & inventory MD 18:221
Jeremiah, of Hingham, 1754 will MD 20:101
Mathew, of Hingham, 1764 will & inventory MD 18:224
SPROUT
Ebenezer (Lt.), of Middleboro, 1726 will MD 25:127
Elizabeth & Mary, of Middleboro, 1726 estate MD 25:70
Robert, of Middleboro, 1711 will & inventory MD 6:8
STANDISH
Alexander, of Duxbury, 1701/2 will & inventory MD 12:99; 1702/3 petition MD 12:176
David, of Pembroke, 1793 will MD 21:71
Desire, of Marshfield, 1723 will & inventory MD 12:48
Ebenezer, of Plympton, 1748 inventory MD 15:125
Hannah, of Hanover, 1801 will MD 21:72
Ichabod, of Halifax, 1763 will MD 15:190
Miles, of Duxbury, 1739 will MD 15:123, 23:133
Moses, of Halifax, 1769 will MD 15:126
Penelope, of Duxbury, 1740 inventory & estate MD 15:125, 23:135
Zachariah, of Plympton, 1770 estate MD 20:16
STAPLE
Seth, of Taunton, 1763 will MD 19:34
STETSON/STUDSON
William, of Scituate, 1699 estate MD 34:54

STEPHENS
  Edward, of Plymouth, 1756 will PN&Q 5:98
STRANGE
  Sarah, of Boston, 1711 estate MD 20:40
STURGIS
  Edward Jr., of Yarmouth, 1694 estate MD 23:61
  Edward Sr., of Yarmouth, 1695 estate MD 27:37
STURTEVANT
  Samuel (Deacon), of Halifax, 1735/6 will PN&Q 5:124
SUNDERLAND
  John, of Eastham, 1700 will MD 17:100
SUTTON
  John Sr., of Scituate, 1691 will MD 31:64, GEN ADV 2:104-105; guardianships GEN ADV 3:91
SWIFT
  Jireh, of Wareham, 1744 will MD 23:40
  William Jr., of Sandwich, 1700 will MD 30:112
  William Sr., of Sandwich, 1705 will MD 30:113
TABER
  Philip, of Dartmouth, 1692/3 inventory MD 16:226
  Thomas (Capt.), of Dartmouth, 1723 will MD 16:231
TAYLOR
  John, of Boston, 1703 will MD 21:122
  John, of Milton, 1748 will MD 21:122
  Sarah, of Barnstable, 1695 inventory MD 24:63
THACHER
  John (Col.), of Yarmouth, 1713 will MD 22:110
  Peter, of Yarmouth, 1735/6 will MD 19:66
  Thankful, of Yarmouth, 1745 will MD 25:99
THAXTER
  David, of Hingham, 1749 will MD 23:147
  Samuel, of Hingham, 1723 will MD 23:146
THAYER
  Ephraim, of Braintree, 1755 will MD 18:113
THOMAS
  Jeremiah, of Middleboro, 1735 will MD 20:132
  John, of Marshfield, 1691/2 inventory MD 31:64, GEN ADV 2:104
THOMPSON see TOMSON
TILDEN
  Benjamin, of Scituate, 1693 inventory GEN ADV 3:92
TINKHAM
  Ebenezer Sr., of Middleboro, 1718 will MD 17:164
  Ephraim Jr., of Middleboro, 1713 inventory MD 17:163
  Ephraim, of Middleboro, 1714 will MD 17:162

TINKHAM con't
Helkiah, of Plymouth, 1716 will MD 12:145
Isaac, of Plymouth, 1708/9 will MD 17:166
TOBEY
Ephraim, of Sandwich, 1693 inventory MD 19:45
TOMKINS
Samuel, of Bridgewater, 1695 will GEN ADV 4:91
TOMSON
Abigail, of Halifax, 1739 will MD 25:21
Ebenezer, of Plymouth, 1726/7 estate MD 25:59
Jacob, of Middleboro, 1726 estate MD 24:168
John Sr. (Lt.), of Middleboro, 1696 will & inventory MD 4:22 & 19:95
John, of Middleboro, 1724 will MD 20:160
Mary, of Halifax, 1756 will MD 25:185
Mercy, of Halifax, 1756 estate MD 19:135
Peter, of Plympton, 1726 estate MD 25:56
Peter, of Plympton, 1731 estate MD 22:136
Thomas, of Halifax, 1742 estate MD 25:177
TUPPER
Hannah, of Middleboro, 1766 will MD 21:101
Ichabod, of Middleboro, 1748 will MD 21:100
TURNER
Elisha, of Scituate, 1700 will MD 32:75
Elizabeth, of Scituate, 1710 will MD 32:77
Ephraim, of Scituate, 1694 administration GEN ADV 3:89, 3:111
George, of Bridgewater, 1695 administration GEN ADV 4:92
Japhet, of Duxbury, 1710/11 estate MD 21:98
John Sr., of Scituate, 1695 will & inventory MD 5:41
Jonathan, of Scituate, 1723 will MD 20:85
Nathan, of Scituate, 1694 administration GEN ADV 3:112
VAUGHAN
George Sr., of Middleboro, 1694 will MD 18:116, GEN ADV 4:88
WADSWORTH
Abigail, of Duxbury, 1723 inventory MD 9:247
John, of Duxbury, 1700 will MD 9:246
John, of Duxbury, 1750 estate MD 21:90
WALLEY
John, of Boston, 1702 administration MD 10:76
WARREN
Benjamin (Capt.), of Plymouth, 1745 will MD 23:152
Elizabeth, of Plymouth, 1747 estate MD 25:13

WARREN con't
James, of Plymouth, 1709 estate MD 21:79
James (Capt.), of Plymouth, 1711/2 will MD 25:6
Mary, of Plymouth, 1795 estate MD 25:14
Mercy, of Plymouth, 1747 estate MD 25:13
Nathaniel, of Plymouth, 1707 will MD 22:44
Richard, of Middleboro, 1696/7 estate MD 21:78
Samuel, of Middleboro, 1750 will MD 21:105

WASHBURN
James, of Bridgewater, 1747 will MD 16:52
Jonathan, of Bridgewater, 1725 estate MD 16:50
Noah, of Bridgewater, 1717 estate MD 24:44
Samuel (Sgt.), of Bridgewater, 1720 will MD 16:49
Thomas, of Bridgewater, 1729/30 will MD 16:51

WATERMAN
Joseph, of Marshfield, 1709 will MD 24:147
Robert, of Halifax, 1744 will MD 22:126

WEBB
Christopher, of Braintree, 1694 will PN&Q 2:52

WEST
Francis, of Duxbury, 1693 administration GEN ADV 3:91

WESTON
Edmund, of Plympton, 1727 estate MD 24:20
Elnathan, of Duxbury, 1728 will MD 15:188

WHISTONE
John, of Scituate, 1693 administration GEN ADV 3:92, 111

WHITE
Cornelius, of Marshfield, 1754 will MD 20:63
Daniel, of Marshfield, 1721 will MD 20:62
Daniel (Capt.), of Marshfield, 1785 will MD 28:29
Hannah, of Marshfield, 1767 will MD 20:66
Jonathan, of Yarmouth, 1736 will MD 9:122
Joseph, of Yarmouth, 1775 will MD 9:123
Joseph, of Yarmouth, 1800 will MD 9:123
Joseph, of Yarmouth, 1816 will MD 9:124
Peregrine, of Marshfield, 1704 will & inventory MD 1:129 or 3:119 (he came on the *Mayflower*)
Peregrine, of Yarmouth, 1833 will MD 9:124
Samuel, of Marshfield, 1786 will MD 28:32
William, of Dartmouth, 1768 will MD 22:8
William, of Dartmouth, 1777 will MD 22:10

WILCOX
Daniel, of Tiverton, 1702 will & inventory MD 16:239
Edward, of Tiverton, 1718 will MD 20:151

WILLARD
  Simon, of Boston, 1709 will MD 10:77
WILLIAMS
  Abiel, of Raynham, 1825 will MD 23:33
  Emanuell, of Taunton, 1719 inventory MD 21:136
  John, of Scituate, 1691 will GEN ADV 4:25
  Joseph, of Taunton, 1693 inventory GEN ADV 4:124
  Nathaniel (Deacon), of Taunton, 1692 inventory
    MD 22:60
  Nathaniel, of Taunton, 1726 will MD 23:2
  Nathaniel, of Raynham, 1775 will MD 23:7
  Thomas, of Eastham, 1692 will MD 31:106
WILLIS
  John Sr., of Bridgewater, 1692 will GEN ADV 3:93
WING
  Daniel, of Sandwich, 1698 will MD 32:133
  John, of Harwich, 1696 will MD 33:173
WINSLOW
  Edward, of Boston, 1680 will & inventory MD 10:53
  Edward, of Boston, 1748 will MD 10:107
  Isaac, of Marshfield, 1736 will MD 24:30
  John, of Boston, 1683 will & inventory MD 10:54
  John, of Boston, 1690 will MD 10:55
  Joseph, of Boston, 1679 administration MD 10:52
  Mary, of Boston, 1676 will & inventory MD 1:65
    (she came on the _Mayflower_)
  Richard, of Boston, 1697 will MD 10:55
  Samuel, of Boston, 1682 will MD 10:52
  Samuel, of Boston, 1745 administration MD 10:106
  Sarah, of Marshfield, 1753 will MD 24:33
  William, of Boston, 1746 administration MD 10:106
WISWALL
  Ichabod (Rev.), of Duxbury, 1700 will & inventory
    MD 19:2
WOOD
  James, of Middleboro, 1728 estate & inventory
    MD 18:229
WORMALL
  Grace, of Duxbury, 1748 will MD 9:249
WRIGHT
  Adam, of Plympton, 1723 will & inventory MD 4:239;
    1723 will MD 11:242
  Isaac, of Plympton, 1760 will MD 21:53
YOUNG
  Abigail, of Eastham, 1692 will MD 15:79

KEY TO ABBREVIATED TITLES

MOST TOWN HISTORIES and compendiums such as SAVAGE were published before the 1930s, when the era of scientific genealogy began, and should be used with caution. Some of the most flagrant errors have been noted in square brackets in entries in this Guide.

Some books listed below were still in print as this volume went to the printer. Other books may be available in used condition. The section which follows this Key lists some publishers and book dealers.

AMERICAN COLONISTS BY COLDHAM
  Coldham, Peter Wilson
English Estates of American Colonists...1610-1699. Baltimore, 1980. GPC.

AMERICAN COLONISTS BY SHERWOOD
  Sherwood, George
American Colonists in English Records. London 1932-1933, reprint Baltimore, 1969. GPC.

ASPINWALL RECS
  [Aspinwall Notarial Records] _A Report of the Record Commissioners of the City of Boston_, vol. 32. Boston MA, 1903.

BANKS ENGLISH ANCESTRY
  Banks, Charles E.
The English Ancestry and Homes of the Pilgrim Fathers.... New York, 1929, reprint Baltimore, 1962, etc. GPC.

BARBADOS PR
Sanders, Joanne McRee
Barbados Records: Wills and Administrations. 3 vols., Houston TX, 1979-1981. Sanders Hist. Pub.

BARNSTABLE CO PR
Unpublished Barnstable County MA Probate Records. Original record books at Registry of Probate, Barnstable MA, or see LDS microfilm.

BARNSTABLE FAMS
Swift, C. F.
Genealogical Notes of Barnstable Families, Being a Reprint of the Amos Otis Papers. Barnstable MA, 1888-1890; reprint Baltimore, 1979. GPC.

BRIDGEWATER BY MITCHELL
Mitchell, Nahum
History of the Early Settlement of Bridgewater...Including an Extensive Family Register. Boston MA, 1840; reprint Bridgewater MA, 1897, Baltimore, 1970. Nourse.

BRISTOL CO PR
Unpublished Bristol County MA Probate Records. Original papers and record books at Registry of Probate, Taunton MA, or see LDS microfilm.

CAMBRIDGE BY PAIGE
Paige, Lucius R.
History of Cambridge 1630-1877. With a Genealogical Register. Boston and New York, 1877.

CAPE COD HIST
Freeman, Frederick
History of Cape Cod. 2 vols. Boston, 1858-62; reprint Yarmouth Port MA, 1965. Parnassus Imprints.

CHATHAM BY SMITH
Smith, William C.
A History of Chatham Mass. 4 parts. Hyannis MA, 1909-1947; reprint Yarmouth Port MA 1971. Parnassus Imprints.

CHARLESTOWN BY WYMAN
Wyman, Thomas B.
The Genealogies and Estates of Charlestown [MA].... 2 vols. Boston, 1879; reprint Somersworth NH, 1982. New England History Press.

DSGR
Magazine of the Detroit Society for Genealogical Research. Vol. 1-- 1937--. Published at Detroit 1983. DSGR.

DUXBURY BY WINSOR
Winsor, Justin
History of the Town of Duxbury, Mass. with Genealogical Registers. Boston MA, 1849; reprint Boston, 1970.

DUXBURY RECS
Etheridge, George
Copy of the Old Records of the Town of Duxbury, Mass. from 1642 to 1770. Plymouth MA, 1893.

EARLY REHOBOTH
Bowen, Richard L.
Early Rehoboth. 4 vols. Rehoboth MA, 1945-1950.

FAMS OF PILGRIMS
Shaw, Hubert K.
Families of the Pilgrims. Boston MA, 1956; revised reprints of each of the 23 families 1981-- MSMD.

GEN ADV
Greenlaw, Lucy H., editor.
The Genealogical Advertiser, a quarterly magazine of family history. Vols. 1-4, 1898-1901; reprint Baltimore, 1974. GPC.

HARVARD GRADS
Sibley, John L.
Biographical sketches of graduates of Harvard University in Cambridge, Mass. Cambridge, vol. 1-- 1873--.

HINGHAM BY LINCOLN
Lincoln, George
History of the Town of Hingham, Mass. Published by the town. Hingham, 1892. Vols. 2 and 3 reprinted, Somersworth NH, 1982. New England History Press.

LDS microfilm
Available for use for a small fee through regional libraries operated by the Genealogical Society of Utah, the genealogical arm of the Church of Jesus Christ of Latter Day Saints, 50 East North Temple, Salt Lake City UT 84150.

LECHFORD'S NOTEBOOK
Lechford, Thomas
Note-book kept by Thomas Lechford, Esq., Lawyer, in Boston, Massachusetts Bay, from June 27, 1638 to July 29, 1641. Cambridge MA, 1885, also vol. 7, Transactions and Collections of the American Antiquarian Society.

LITTLE COMPTON FAMS
Wilbour, Benjamin F.
Little Compton Families Published by the Little Compton Historical Society from Records Compiled by Benjamin F. Wilbour. Providence RI, 1967.

MA PIONEERS
Pope, Charles H.
The Pioneers of Massachusetts.... Boston MA, 1900; reprint Baltimore, 1965. GPC.

MARSHFIELD BY RICHARDS
Richards, Lysander S.
History of Marshfield, Mass., with genealogy. 2 vols. Plymouth MA, 1901-1905.

MARSHFIELD VR
Sherman, Robert M. and Ruth W.
Vital Records of Marshfield, Massachusetts to the Year 1850. Warwick RI 1969; reprint 1980. RIMD.

MARTHA'S VINEYARD BY BANKS
Banks, Charles E.
History of Martha's Vineyard, with Genealogy. 3 vols. Boston MA, 1911-25; reprint Edgartown MA, 1966.

MASS BAY RECS
Shurtleff, Nathaniel B.
Records of the Governor and Company of the Massachusetts Bay in New England. 5 vols. in 6. Boston MA, 1853-4; reprint New York, 1971.

MAY RDR
Bowman, George E.
The Mayflower Reader: A Selection of Articles From The Mayflower Descendant. Baltimore, 1978. GPC.

MD
Bowman, George E., editor.
The Mayflower Descendant: A Quarterly Magazine of Pilgrim History and Genealogy. 34 vols. Boston MA, 1899-1937. MSMD. Available on microfiche through GSMD.

ME HGR
Watson, S.M.
Maine Historical and Genealogical Recorder. 9 vols., Portland ME, 1884-1898; reprint in 3 vols., Baltimore, 1973. GPC.

MF 1
Kellogg, Lucy Mary, editor.
Mayflower Families Through Five Generations: Descendants of the Pilgrims who Landed at Plymouth, Mass. December 1620. Families: Francis Eaton, Samuel Fuller and William White. Plymouth MA, 1975. GSMD.

MF 2
Sherman, Robert M., editor.
Mayflower Families Through Five Generations:...Families: James Chilton, Richard More and Thomas Rogers. Plymouth MA, 1979. GSMD.

MF 3
Harding, Anne Borden, editor.
Mayflower Families Through Five Generations:...Family: George Soule. Plymouth MA, 1980. GSMD.

MIDDLEBORO BY WESTON
Weston, Thomas
History of the Town of Middleboro [MA]. Boston MA, 1906; reprint Taunton MA, 1975. GBIP vendor #665.

MQ
The Mayflower Quarterly.
Published by the General Society of Mayflower Descendants, Plymouth MA. Vol. 1-- 1935--. GSMD.

NARRA HIST REG
Arnold, James N., editor.
Narragansett Historical Register: A Magazine Devoted to the Antiquities, Genealogy and Historical Matter...of the State of Rhode Island. Vol. 1-9, 1882-1891.

NEHGR
New England Historical and Genealogical Register. Vol. 1-- Jan. 1847--. Published by the New England Historic Genealogical Society, Boston MA. NEHGS.

NGSQ
National Genealogical Society Quarterly. Vol. 1-- 1912--. Published by the National Genealogical Society, Washington DC. NGS.

PLYM ANC LANDMARKS
Davis, William T.
Ancient Landmarks of Plymouth. 2nd edition 1899; reprint of Part Two under title Genealogical Register of Plymouth Families. Baltimore, 1975. GPC.

PLYM CH RECS
Plymouth Church Records, 1620-1859. 2 vols. New York, 1920-23; reprint Baltimore, 1975. GPC.

PLYM CO CT RECS
Konig, David T.
Plymouth [County] Court Records 1686-1859. 16 vols. 1978-1981. Wilmington DE. Michael Glazier.

PLYM CO PR
Unpublished Plymouth County MA Probate Records. Original papers and record books at Registry of Probate, Plymouth MA, or see LDS microfilm.

PLYM COL LR
Unpublished Plymouth Colony Land Records. See LDS microfilm.

PLYM COL MARR
Wakefield, Robert S.
Plymouth Colony Marriages to 1650 together with Mary Chilton's Title to Celebrity. Warwick RI 1978; reprint 1980. RIMD.

PLYM COL PR
Unpublished Plymouth Colony Probate Records. See LDS microfilm.

PLYM COL RECS
Shurtleff, Nathaniel B. and Pulsifer, David
Records of the Colony of New Plymouth in New England. 12 vols., Boston MA, 1855-61; reprint 12 vols. in 6, New York, 1968. [Volume 8 reprinted 1976 by GPC.]

PLYM SCRAP
Pope, Charles H.
The Plymouth Scrapbook: The Oldest Original Documents Extant in Plymouth Archives.... Boston MA, 1918. Goodspeed.

PLYM TR
Records of the Town of Plymouth. 3 vols. Plymouth MA, 1889-1903.

PN&Q
Bowman, George E., editor.
Pilgrim Notes and Queries. 5 vols. Boston MA, 1913-1917. MSMD.

REHOBOTH see EARLY REHOBOTH

REHOBOTH VR
Arnold, James N.
Vital Record of Rehoboth, 1642-1896. Marriages, Intentions, Births, Deaths.... Providence RI, 1897.

RI FAMS
Genealogies of Rhode Island Families from Rhode Island Periodicals. 2 vols. Baltimore, 1983. GPC.

RI GEN DICT
Austin, John O.
The Genealogical Dictionary of Rhode Island, comprising Three Generations of Settlers who came before 1690. Albany NY, 1887; reprint of annotated copy (owned by Rhode Island Historical Society) Cleveland OH, 1967 and Baltimore, 1969. GPC.

RIGR
Rhode Island Genealogical Register. Vol. 1-- 1978--. Published at East Princeton MA in 1983. RIGR.

RI ROOTS
Rhode Island Roots. Vol. 1-- 1975--. Published at Warwick RI in 1983. RIGS.

RIVR
Arnold, James N. Vital Record of Rhode Island, 1636-1850. 21 vols. Providence RI, 1891-1912; reprint of VR of some towns in vols. 1 and 2, 1982. Hunterdon House.

SAVAGE
Savage, James
A Genealogical Dictionary of the First Settlers of New England, Showing Three Generations of Those Who came before May 1692.... 4 vols. Boston MA, 1860-62; reprint Baltimore, 1965. GPC.

SCITUATE BY DEANE
Deane, Samuel
History of Scituate, Mass., from its Settlement to 1831. Boston MA, 1831; reprint No. Scituate MA, 1899 and 1975. Scituate Hist. Soc.

SCITUATE BY PRATT
Pratt, Harvey H.
The Early Planters of Scituate. Rockland MA, 1929. Scituate Hist. Soc.

SUFFOLK CO PR
Original 17th century documents and record books at the Suffolk Co. court house, Boston MA.

SWANSEA HIST
Wright, Otis O.
History of Swansea Mass. 1667-1917. Swansea, 1917.

SWANSEA TR BOOK A
Mason, Alverdo H.
Book A, Records of the Town of Swansea [MA] 1662 to 1705. East Braintree MA, 1900.

TAG
The American Genealogist. Vol. 1-- 1922--. Published at Des Moines IA in 1983. TAG.

TG
The Genealogist. Vol. 1-- 1980--. Published at New York City in 1983. TG.

TORREY'S MARRIAGES
Torrey, Clarence A.
New England Marriages Prior to 1700. Manuscript at NEHGS; also available on microfilm, 7 rolls. 1952. NEHGS.

WATERS
Waters, Henry F.
Genealogical Gleanings in England: Abstracts of Wills relating to Early American families...with New Series. 2 vols. 1901; reprint Salem MA 1907 (with new series added); reprint Baltimore, 1969. GPC.

WEYMOUTH BY CHAMBERLAIN
Chamberlain, G.W.
History of Weymouth with Genealogies.... 4 vols. Boston MA, 1923.

WINTHROP'S JOURNAL
Hosmer, James K. editor
History of New England 1630-1649. 2 vols. New York, 1908; reprint New York, 1966.

YARMOUTH BY SWIFT
Swift, Charles F.
History of Old Yarmouth...and Dennis [MA]...to 1876. Yarmouth Port MA, 1884; reprint Yarmouth Port MA, 1975. Parnassus Imprints.

YARMOUTH MA VR
Sherman, Robert M. and Ruth W. Sherman
Vital Records of Yarmouth, Massachusetts to the Year 1850. 2 vols. Warwick RI, 1975.

WHERE TO OBTAIN BOOKS AND JOURNALS

Publishers

ADDRESSES OF PUBLISHERS of many of the books and journals listed in our Key to Abbreviated Titles, which are still in print, are given below.

DSGR--Detroit Society for Genealogical Research, c/o Burton Historical Collection, Detroit Public Library, 5201 Woodward Avenue, Detroit MI 48202

GBIP--Genealogical Books in Print, 6818 Lois Dr., Springfield VA 22150.

GPC--Genealogical Publishing Co., 111 Water St., Baltimore MD 21202

GSMD--General Society of Mayflower Descendants, PO Box 297, Plymouth MA 02361

Hunterdon House--38 Swan Street, Lambertville NJ 08530

Michael Glazier--1210A King Street, Wilmington DE 19801

MSMD--Massachusetts Society of Mayflower Descendants, 101 Newbury St., Boston MA 02116

NEHGS--New England Historic Genealogical Society, 101 Newbury St., Boston MA 02116

New England History Press--PO Box 70, Somersworth NH 03878

NGS--National Genealogical Society, 1921 Sunderland Place NW, Washington DC 20036

Nourse--Mrs. Leo F. Nourse, Box 44, Bridgewater MA 02324

Parnassus Imprints--Route 6A, Yarmouth Port MA 02675

PCRG--Plymouth Colony Research Group, 128 Massasoit Drive, Warwick RI 02888

RIGR--Rhode Island Genealogical Register, PO Box 585, East Princeton MA 01517

RIGS--Rhode Island Genealogical Society, PO Box 7618, Warwick RI 02887-7618

RIMD--Rhode Island Mayflower Descendants, 128 Massasoit Drive, Warwick RI 02888

Sanders Historical Publications--13603 Pebblebrook, Houston TX 77079

Scituate Hist. Soc.--Scituate MA 02066

TAG--The American Genealogist, 1232 39th Street, Des Moines IA 50311

TG--The Genealogist, PO Box 1058, Rockefeller Center Station, New York NY 10185

Book Dealers

MANY COMPANIES sell genealogical books. Those listed below are probably the largest and best known.

Genealogical Publishing Co. (GPC), 111 Water Street, Baltimore MD 21202: Sells new and used books; free catalog.

Genealogical Books in Print (GBIP), 6818 Lois Dr., Springfield VA 22150: Publishes a bibliography, _Genealogical and Local History Books in Print_; $16 for paperback edition. Some listed items can be ordered through the same address.

Goodspeed's Book Shop Inc., 7 Beacon St., Boston MA 02108: Sells new and used books; $3 for catalog.

Tuttle Antiquarian Books Inc., 28 South Main St., Rutland VT 05701: Sells new and used books; $4 for catalog.

Xerox University Microfilms, 300 North Zeeb Rd., Ann Arbor MI 48106: Many out-of-print books and magazines are available via Xerox or microfilm copies produced under their "On Demand Book Program." Available only to libraries. Catalog.

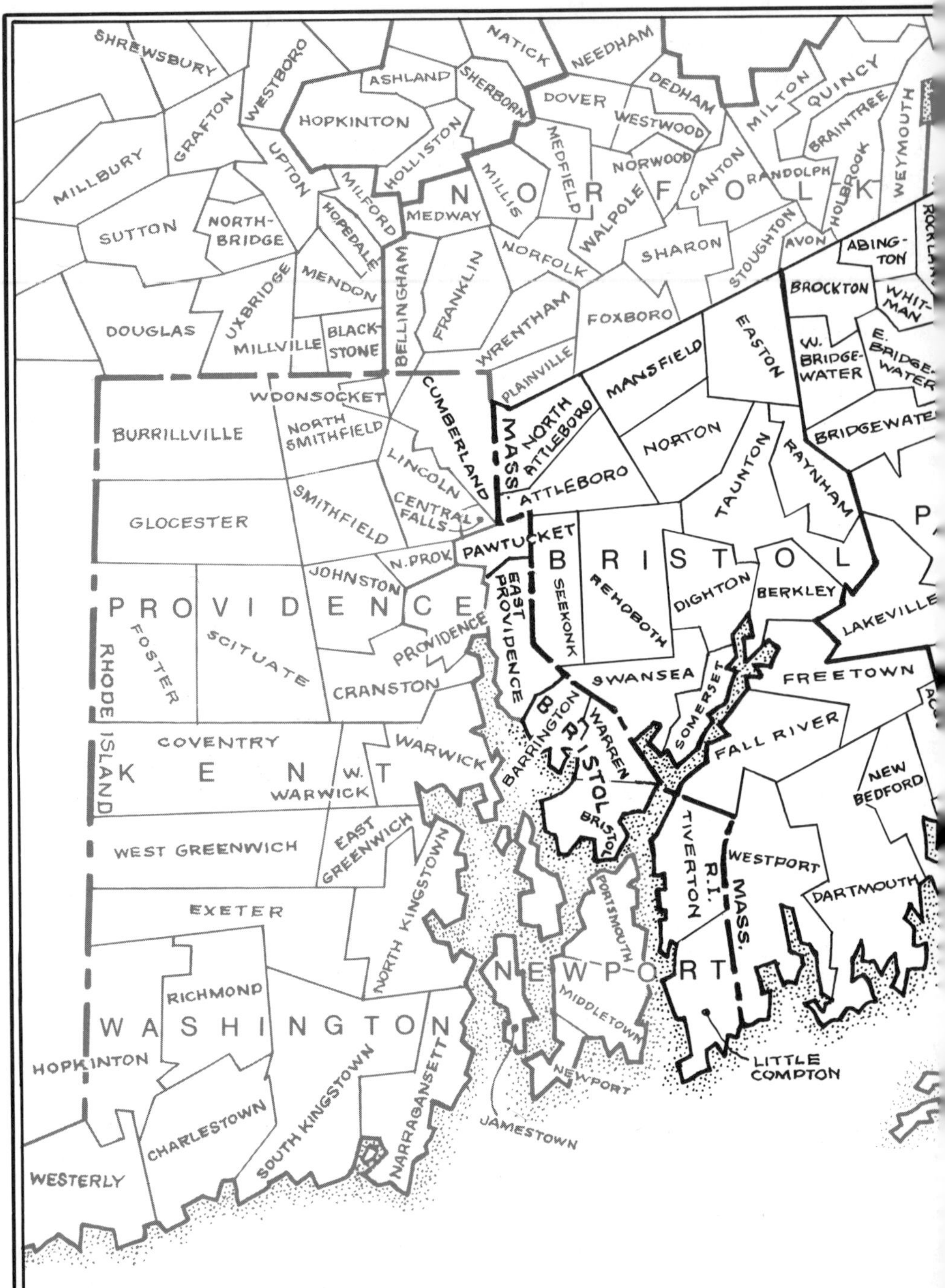

1980 BOUNDARIES OF PRESENT DAY TOWNS IN WHAT W